Intelligent Data Analysis for e-Learning

Intelligent Data Analysis for e-Learning
Enhancing Security and Trustworthiness in Online Learning Systems

Jorge Miguel
San Jorge University, Spain

Santi Caballé
Universitat Oberta de Catalunya, Spain

Fatos Xhafa
Universitat Politècnica de Catalunya, Spain

Series Editor Fatos Xhafa
Universitat Politècnica de Catalunya, Spain

AMSTERDAM · BOSTON · HEIDELBERG · LONDON
NEW YORK · OXFORD · PARIS · SAN DIEGO
SAN FRANCISCO · SINGAPORE · SYDNEY · TOKYO
Academic Press is an imprint of Elsevier

Academic Press is an imprint of Elsevier
125 London Wall, London EC2Y 5AS, United Kingdom
525 B Street, Suite 1800, San Diego, CA 92101-4495, United States
50 Hampshire Street, 5th Floor, Cambridge, MA 02139, United States
The Boulevard, Langford Lane, Kidlington, Oxford OX5 1GB, United Kingdom

Notices
Knowledge and best practice in this field are constantly changing. As new research and experience
broaden our understanding, changes in research methods, professional practices, or medical
treatment may become necessary.

Practitioners and researchers must always rely on their own experience and knowledge in evaluating
and using any information, methods, compounds, or experiments described herein. In using such
information or methods they should be mindful of their own safety and the safety of others, including
parties for whom they have a professional responsibility.

To the fullest extent of the law, neither the Publisher nor the authors, contributors, or editors, assume
any liability for any injury and/or damage to persons or property as a matter of products liability,
negligence or otherwise, or from any use or operation of any methods, products, instructions, or
ideas contained in the material herein.

Library of Congress Cataloging-in-Publication Data
A catalog record for this book is available from the Library of Congress

British Library Cataloguing-in-Publication Data
A catalogue record for this book is available from the British Library

ISBN: 978-0-12-804535-0

For information on all Academic Press publications
visit our website at https://www.elsevier.com/

Working together
to grow libraries in
developing countries

www.elsevier.com • www.bookaid.org

Publisher: Todd Green
Acquisition Editor: Brian Romer
Editorial Project Manager: Amy Invernizzi
Production Project Manager: Priya Kumaraguruparan
Cover Designer: Victoria Pearson

Typeset by SPi Global, India

To our families

Contents

List of Figures

List of Tables

Foreword

In the current fast evolution of Internet technologies, big data analytics have emerged as the *de facto* process to manage and analyze large data sets with countless applications to many scientific and social domains. Learning Analytics is purposely focused on addressing the demanding needs of processing and analyzing large learning data sets to provide e-Learning professors, managers, and stakeholders with meaningful knowledge for improving educational activities, monitoring of courses, and the learning process as a whole. In this context high performance computing (HPC) and distributed computing techniques are becoming more necessary to support efficient data processing and analysis from large and unstructured data sets arising from heterogeneous online educational systems and services involving thousands of students, teachers, and staff.

The current book *Intelligent Data Analysis for e-Learning: Enhancing Security and Trustworthiness in Online Learning Systems* is an excellent application of the above topics for the provision of information security and trustworthiness for e-Learning processes, thus guaranteeing fairness, reliability, and integrity of online assessment activities. The volume shows an impressive combination of methodologies and technological approaches to tackle security issues in e-Learning by leveraging both trustworthiness models based on peer-to-peer (P2P) trust in collaborative learning scenarios and popular distributed computing techniques, such as Hadoop and MapReduce for massive parallel data processing. The authors provide excellent guidelines to handle the many issues and challenges involved in e-Learning in order to effectively monitor online students over time throughout their learning progression and detect anomalous behavior during e-assessment activities. A number of case studies and evaluations of real-world e-Learning scenarios are provided throughout the volume, which present an excellent demonstration of the successful use of the multidisciplinary and complex approaches presented in an easy and very practical way.

This book delivers on its research objectives by thoroughly investigating a number of timely topics comprising trustworthy computing, security, e-Learning analytics, and massive parallel data processing for e-Learning. I believe that the list of topics explored here, coupled with the findings, lessons learned, and challenges identified will make the readers think of the implications of such new ideas on innovative developments for online education.

The publication of *Intelligent Data Analysis for e-Learning: Enhancing Security and Trustworthiness in Online Learning Systems* is a valuable achievement and an important contribution to e-Learning, massive data processing, and analysis literature, and in particular to these emerging topics when applied to online education.

I would like to commend the authors on such an achievement and wish that the readers find the book useful and hopefully a source of inspiration for more research ideas.

A.Y. Zomaya
Chair Professor of High Performance Computing & Networking
University of Sydney
Australia

Acknowledgments

This research was partly funded by the Spanish Government through the following projects: TIN2011-27076-C03-02 "CO-PRIVACY"; CONSOLIDER INGENIO 2010 CSD 2007-0004 "ARES"; TIN2013-45303-P "ICT-FLAG" Enhancing ICT education through Formative assessment, Learning Analytics and Gamification; and by funds from the Spanish Ministry for Economy and Competitiveness (MINERS) and the European Union (FENDER funds) under grant COMMAS (ref. TIN2013-46181-C2-1-R).

Introduction

1

Information and communication technologies (ICE) have been widely adopted and exploited in most educational institutions in order to support e-Learning through different learning methodologies, ICE solutions, and design paradigms. In particular, over the past decade computer-supported collaborative learning (CSCL) has become one of the most influential learning paradigms devoted to improving teaching and learning with the help of modern information and communication technology [1]. In order to support CSCL implementation, many learning management systems (LMSs) have appeared in the marketplace and the e-Learning stakeholders (ie, e-Learning designers and managers, tutors, and students) are increasingly demanding new requirements. Among these requirements, information security (IS) is a significant factor involved in CSCL processes deployed in LMSs, which determines the accurate development of CSCL activities. However, according to Weippl [2] and Eibl [3] CSCL services are usually designed and implemented without much consideration for security aspects.

The lack of security in e-Learning is also supported by practical and real attacks in ICE. As a matter of fact, recent attack reports [4,5] have demonstrated a significant amount of real-life security attacks experienced by organizations and educational institutions. The CyberSecurity Watch Survey is a cooperative survey research conducted by leading companies and educational institutions [4]. This report reveals that security attacks are a reality for most organizations: 81% of respondents' organizations have experienced a security event (ie, an adverse event that threatens some aspect of security).

Since LMS are software packages that integrate tools that support CSCL activities, technological vulnerabilities have to be considered. Recent security reports [4,5] have shown how Web application servers and database management systems, which usually support LMS infrastructure, are deployed with security flaws. Dealing with more technological details related to LMSs, the Trustwave Global Security Report shows how Web application servers and database management systems are deployed with security vulnerabilities [5]. Moreover potential LMS attacks can be studied by analyzing their specific security vulnerabilities. For instance, in Moodle Security Announcements [6], 49 serious vulnerabilities were reported in 2013.

Intelligent Data Analysis for e-Learning. http://dx.doi.org/10.1016/B978-0-12-804535-0.00001-0

Regarding security in educational institutions in the scope of Spanish universities, the RedIRIS Computer Emergency Response Team is aimed at the early detection of security incidents affecting their affiliated institutions. As stated in [7], the total number of incidents received was 10,028 and this value represents an increase of 74.15% compared to the previous year. In the same context, in [8], the authors stated that only 17% of Spanish universities have adopted the application of the Spanish National Security Framework and only 18% of students use digital certificates. Although it might seem that these plans and initiatives are related to security in e-Learning, they are actually focused on secure e-Administration and management. In contrast, e-Learning security, which can determine these management processes, is not usually considered. For instance, a student who is able to obtain a course certificate following advanced security techniques, such as a digital signature, may find the same security level is not required when performing e-Assessment activities.

One of the key issues in IS is that security drawbacks cannot be solved with technology solutions alone [9]. To date, even the most advanced security technological solutions, such as public key infrastructure (PKI) have drawbacks that impede the development of complete and overall technological security frameworks. Even most advanced PKI solutions have vulnerabilities that impede the development of a highly secure framework. For this reason, this proposal suggests research into enhancing technological security models with functional approaches.

Among functional approaches, trustworthiness analysis, modeling, assessment, and prediction methods are suitable in the context of CSCL. Trustworthiness can be considered as a suitable functional factor in CSCL because most trustworthiness models are based on peer-to-peer (P2P) interactions [10,11] and CSCL is closely related to students' interaction. Although some trustworthiness methods have been proposed and investigated, these approaches have been little investigated in CSCL with the aim of enhancing security properties. Therefore this book proposes to conduct research on security in CSCL by enhancing technological security solutions with trustworthiness and through experimenting with methods, techniques, and trustworthiness models, to eventually arrange a trustworthiness methodology approach for collaborative e-Learning.

In addition to security applications based on trustworthiness, other CSCL enhancements related to pedagogical factors can also be considered. According to Hussain et al. [12] the existence of trust reduces the perception of risk, which in turn improves the behavior in the interaction and willingness to engage in the interaction. In the context of CSCL, interaction between students is one of the most relevant factors in learning performance. Therefore trustworthiness is directly related to CSCL and can enhance the performance of collaborative learning activities. In contrast, IS can encourage and endorse trustworthiness, but IS does not directly endow learning enhancement. Another significant difference between IS and trustworthiness, with respect to CSCL, is the dynamic nature of trustworthiness [13]. Student behavior is dynamic and it evolves during the CSCL process. While security is static regarding student behavior, trustworthiness also evolves and its assessment can be adapted to student and group behavior changes.

A CSCL activity is a general concept that can involve very different cases, actors, processes, requirements, and learning objectives in the complex context of e-Learning [14]. To alleviate this complexity we limit our application scope in specific CSCL activities, namely, we focus on online collaborative assessment (collaborative e-Assessment). General e-Assessment processes offer enormous opportunities to enhance the student learning experience, such as delivering on-demand tests, providing electronic marking, and immediate feedback on tests [15]. In higher education e-Assessment is typically employed to deliver formative tests to the students. In terms of reported unethical conduct occurring during online exam taking [16], an e-Assessment is an e-Exam with most of the common characteristics of virtual exams. In this book we endow collaborative e-Assessment activities with trustworthiness evaluation and prediction to enhance user security requirements.

The topics discussed so far are addressed to improve the security of CSCL activities with trustworthiness models. In addition to the considerations related to security, CSCL, and trustworthiness, we actually need to incorporate analysis and visualization of P2P systems into the security model so that tutors are presented with, and informed regarding, the results of P2P trustworthiness.

To sum up, the target of this research is an e-Learning system formed by collaborative activities developed in an LMS. The system has to provide security support to carry out these activities and to collect trustworthiness data generated by learning and collaboration processes. Both technological frameworks and online collaborative learning are in line with the e-Learning strategies developed in many educational institutions. In particular, our real e-Learning context of the UOC develops full online education based on collaborative learning activities. Following this institutional view, IS becomes an essential issue to be considered in order for distance universities to develop secure e-Assessment processes and activities on which grades, certificates, and many types of evaluation models may be dependent. The research presented in this book follows this direction and provides solid answers to the formulated research questions.

1.1 OBJECTIVES

The main challenge of the research presented in this book is to build an innovative trustworthiness methodological approach to enhance IS in online collaborative learning. To this end, we defined the following objectives:

- To define a security model based on IS properties and trustworthiness intended to analyze security in CSCL activities by considering specific security requirements.
- To build a comprehensive trustworthiness methodology offering a guideline for the design and management of CSCL activities based on trustworthiness. This objective is composed of two subobjectives:

- to build e-Assessment P2P activities based on the trustworthiness methodology proposed; and
- to propose P2P visualization methods to manage security events in e-Learning activities.
- To provide decision information in order to discover anomalous student behavior that compromises security through trustworthiness evaluation and prediction.
- To design secure CSCL activities based on trustworthiness approaches in terms of LMS components derived from the previous security model, methodologies and decision information on trustworthiness.
- To develop experimental pilots of the previous LMS components with the aim to validate the enhancement of IS in CSCL activities.

In addition to theoretical and design objectives, experimental activities were conducted in real online courses. In the real learning context of the Open University of Catalonia (Universitat Oberta de Catalunya [UOC]), the collaborative learning processes are an essential part of its pedagogical model. Since this paradigm is massively applied to support UOC courses, security requirements can be widely analyzed in this scenario. Therefore the theoretical models have to be tested, evaluated, and verified by experimental pilots incorporated as a part of several real courses of the university.

The above objectives have motivated research on security in online collaborative learning by enhancing technological security solutions based on trustworthiness. The ultimate aim is to build a solid trustworthiness methodology approach for CSCL devoted to offering secure collaborative e-Assessment for students, tutors, and managers.

1.2 BOOK ORGANIZATION

This book is structured as follows. In Chapter 2 we provide an overview of the current developments in the domain of e-Learning, including online collaborative learning, P2P learning, and mobile collaborative systems and applications, which have security as a key requirement. Then, in Chapter 3, we explore trustworthiness and technological security approaches with the aim of establishing security requirements for e-Learning participants and designers. In the next chapter, Chapter 4, we take all the approaches described in the previous chapters one step further and investigate a holistic security approach for online collaborative learning and P2P learning based on an effective trustworthiness model. In Chapter 5 we focus on the issue of handling user trustworthiness information, which involves large amounts of ill-structured data generated by various systems during learning activities. We discuss and propose a parallel processing approach to build relevant information for modeling trustworthiness. We then include two evaluation and validation chapters of the previous trustworthiness-based models and methodologies for secure e-Learning carried out in the real e-Learning context of the UOC, as well as the results of many experiments performed in online collaborative learning and problem-based learning activities in support of P2P and collaborative learning e-Assessment. In particular, Chapter 6 presents the evaluation and validation activities of the previous trustworthiness methodological approach presented in this book. In Chapter 7 we report results related to data collection, processing, and visualization methods. Finally, Chapter 8 highlights the main ideas, models, and findings presented in each chapter and concludes the book by outlining ongoing and future work.

1.3 BOOK READING

The book is organized so as to be self-contained and to facilitate ease of reading by readers from various disciplinary fields including, primarily, those from the fields of e-Learning and CSCL, but also readers from security and trustworthy computing, data analysis, and parallel computing. The chapters are ordered sequentially to facilitate the reading and understanding of ideas, models, and findings presented in the chapters.

Security for e-Learning

2.1 BACKGROUND

Since 1998, student privacy requirements have been considered to be an important factor in e-Learning design and deployment. Privacy requirements for students in e-Learning are an order of magnitude greater than those for students in a more traditional campus environment. In [17] the authors suggested that the most effective mechanism for dealing with student privacy, in the context of the e-Learning environment, should be a task force or committee made up of those who are closely involved in privacy requirements. Subsequent works on e-Learning privacy were focused on specifying and detailing how privacy is involved in, and related to, e-Learning processes. In [18] a policy-based privacy and security management scheme for e-Learning was proposed using a policy language specification. This approach consisted of a policy-based agent coordination for effective collaboration in e-Learning. Furthermore, privacy was analyzed by presenting the basic principles behind privacy practices and legislation, and investigating the more popular e-Learning standards to determine their provisions and limitations for privacy requirements [19], concluding that current e-Learning standards only treat privacy and security superficially.

A different perspective of privacy properties was presented in [20] aiming at collecting requirements of end-users. The findings and conclusions of this study showed how security and privacy levels in e-Learning need to be increased in various areas. Finally, other research works on privacy in e-Learning have been focused on the following challenges and goals:

- to propose a guarantor-mediated reputation and a context-based identity management scheme without requiring specific knowledge of student identities [21];
- to take a risk-driven approach to discussing the real-world operation of a fully-featured learning management system (LMS) from the perspective of privacy management [22];

Intelligent Data Analysis for e-Learning. http://dx.doi.org/10.1016/B978-0-12-804535-0.00002-2

- to track student activities, with an emphasis on privacy threats and data protection [23]; and
- to classify the motivation of privacy invasion within e-Learning and propose security solutions [24].

Beyond student privacy requirements, previous works related to additional security services must be considered. For instance, with respect to digital identity services, as more and more learners are moving to e-Learning, concerns regarding digital identity loss become a big challenge. In the work of Yong [25], the design for a metaformat of digital identities of e-Learning users was presented based on public key infrastructure (PKI) identity services. In [26], issues involved in using PKI technologies to solve security requirements in e-Learning were briefly presented by giving motivations for its development. Other works that consider integration specifications [27,28] provided some appropriate framework to effectively support authentication and authorization services, offering mutual trust to both learners and service providers using attribute-based encryption [28] or general PKI solutions [27]. Finally, research has been done on security issues of presence verification mechanism [15,29] and security services analysis [30,31] in order to specifically examine e-Learning activities, virtual assignments and exams.

From an international e-Learning standards perspective, these greatly help to guarantee security and to develop user confidence and protection, while respecting the legitimate interests of all stakeholders [32]. However, international standards are still far from considering the essential role that security issues have in learning processes. For instance, the instructional management system (IMS) Global Learning Consortium [33] has a series of reference specifications for e-Learning, but very few references regarding security. Indeed, according to IMS [34], the details of the security architecture being employed to support the learner information system is outside the scope of the IMS specifications. Although security specifications are outside this scope, the same specification refers to security in e-Learning as a significant factor in providing mechanisms that can be used to support the implementation of any suitable e-Learning architecture [34].

Some comprehensive security studies in e-Learning were proposed in [2,3], which we briefly discuss next.

In [2] several guidelines are proposed for designing and developing secure e-Learning with special emphasis on organizational and management factors. To this end, the ISO-17799 international security standard [35] is considered. This international standard establishes the guidelines and general principles for initiating, implementing, maintaining, and improving information security (IS) management in organizations. Moreover, a model identifying the most important steps of a risk analysis is proposed as follows:

1. *Identification of assets.* For most e-Learning projects, a qualitative risk analysis is a suitable method because it requires little effort and the results are

sufficiently precise. Although the advantage of this method is that it is extremely fast, if e-Learning is the focus of a business, more precise methods are required.

2. *Estimation or calculation of threats and risks.* Two basic forms of threat can be distinguished: deliberate threats (eg, attacking a system) and accidental threats (eg, hardware failure). For each asset, a list of threats needs to be compiled and a matrix can be used to organize this process.

3. *Setting priorities.* To set priorities correctly the expected annual damage can be calculated as follows:

$$Expected\_damage = Value\_assets \times Probability\_occurrence. \qquad (2.1)$$

4. *Implementation of controls and countermeasures.* Many countermeasures reduce a risk but do not eliminate it completely. With regard to the estimate of costs, four types of costs have to be considered: damage without countermeasure, damage with countermeasure, costs of the countermeasure, and costs of plan B (alternative plan that can be implemented).

5. *Monitoring of risks and of the effectiveness of countermeasures.* According to Weippl [2], during implementation, the costs of countermeasures should be considered and monitored. This is useful for subsequent projects and improves the accuracy of future implementations. The purpose of the monitoring processes is to compare the costs and the benefits of each measure, as well as to highlight the importance of risk management. Moreover, staff, faculty, and students become aware of the real costs of security design.

This view is closely related to other management models, which focus on the security in information security management systems (ISMSs) [36], providing a model for establishing, implementing, operating, monitoring, reviewing, maintaining, and improving an ISMS. These management solutions complete the risk analysis model proposed. Among these models, the ISO/IEC international standard [37] encourages its users to emphasize the importance of:

1. understanding an organization's IS requirements and the need to establish policy and objectives for IS;
2. implementing and operating controls to manage an organization's security risks in the context of the organization's overall risks;
3. monitoring and reviewing the performance and effectiveness of the ISMS; and
4. continuous improvement based on objective measurement.

However, the above approach has two main limitations when designing secure frameworks for e-Learning. First, although a model for security risk analysis is defined and some security measures are proposed, such as pretty good privacy (PGP) or role-based access control, the approach does not actually conduct a complete analysis and design process. Therefore this model does not provide a systematic methodology for the domain of e-Learning security design. The second limitation is related to the requirements proposed by the security user. The specification includes:

1. protecting learning content copyright of authors;
2. ensuring protection of teachers from students who may undermine their evaluation system by cheating; and
3. protecting students from being too closely monitored by their teachers when using the software.

Although this specification may be useful during initial phases of the analysis, it can hide real needs. This limitation implies the need for a more holistic approach in order to identify a more comprehensive set of security requirements in e-Learning. Therefore as the second aforementioned main reference on security in e-Learning, in [3] the author focused on investigating e-Learning from interdisciplinary perspectives.

The multidisciplinary approach for security in e-Learning presented in [3] is devoted to developing a security concept that provides a sufficient level of security without negatively influencing the learning process. For this purpose, the following research methodology is proposed:

1. *Identification of e-Learning criteria.* This reference suggests that e-Learning is an interdisciplinary field, including educational science with learning psychology and didactics as well as information technologies, such as IS or software engineering. In order to achieve a proper level of security, the impact on security for e-Learning of these different disciplines must be considered and analyzed. Hence, common criteria should be extracted and specific discipline issues need to be examined with respect to mutually influencing research aspects.
2. *Threat analysis and demonstration of case studies.* Criteria and dependencies are considered as starting points for the threat analysis to uncover possible problems and threat situations for e-Learning. A systematic methodology must be applied to guarantee reasonable outcomes for this analysis process.
3. *Development of recommendations.* Topics from educational science are far from being technically manageable for technical deployment, but they build a certain base of requirements to be fulfilled in order to offer secure e-Learning systems. Moreover, models and methods from IS are technically oriented and can restrict the usability of the system only for the sake of security. Therefore it is important to transfer educational and functional requirements to technically manageable aspects in order to find security mechanisms and measures that can be adapted appropriately. Ultimately, the goal of this process is to make recommendations for secure e-Learning systems that can be applied to practical situations and that sufficiently take care of the learning process.

Once the identification criteria is defined a new measure for the assessment of a security rating for an e-Learning system is defined and the security concept of the system is summarized in a single value. The measure only considers the theoretical security, not the actual implementation quality. Therefore results of this measure only deal with the theoretical security, not the real security in the e-Learning development.

In addition to these recommendations for implementing an e-Learning system with an appropriate security level, the same reference also suggests a proxy server solution that acts as a security agent to take over security critical activities from learners without distracting them from the actual learning process. However, the proxy must have access to the private key of the user. Hence, the user's private key will be stored in the server file system and, for example, be embedded into the user's cryptographic smart cards. If this server had a security failure then the digital identity of all users could be faked, even the server itself could be supplanted by an external agent (eg, a man-in-the-middle attack). Therefore we consider these sorts of measures to be unsuitable in the overall context of e-Learning security.

2.2 INFORMATION SECURITY IN e-LEARNING

Information and communication technologies (ICT) have been widely adopted and exploited in most educational institutions in order to support e-Learning through different learning methodologies, ICT solutions, and learning paradigms. Many LMSs have appeared in the marketplace whose stakeholders (ie, e-Learning designers and managers, tutors, and students) increasingly demand new and challenging requirements. Among these requirements, IS is a significant factor involved in the e-Learning services deployed in LMSs, which determines the accurate development of e-Learning activities. However, according to Weippl [2] and Eibl [3] e-Learning services are usually designed and implemented without much consideration for security aspects.

2.2.1 CLASSIFYING SECURITY ATTACKS

Before starting the review of the most common security attacks in e-Learning, we can ask ourselves the following question: Why do we need to understand security attacks? Obviously, the purpose of this research is not to discover how to carry out a security attack and consequently damage a real system but to understand attacks in order to discover the protection mechanisms devoted to protecting e-Learning systems [38].

Recently, many researchers have conducted, and are presently conducting relevant efforts in this field, resulting in a number of taxonomies of security attacks. In [39], through analyzing existing research in attack classification the authors proposed the most comprehensive taxonomies by classifying attacks into three dimensions, as follows:

1. *The sources dimension*: The sources of attack refer to the localities of the attacks. They can be divided into local and remote. Local attacks are initiated from inside the target itself while the remote ones are initiated from outside the target.

2. *The techniques dimension*: The attack techniques are the methods that attackers adopt. Attacks are classified into seven methodologies based on their implementation techniques: infection, exploding, probe, cheat, traverse, concurrency, and others.
3. *The results dimension*: The results of an attack are classified into four categories: no category, information disclosure, rights escalation, and harm implementation.

Besides attack sources, techniques, or results, further attacks of any kind that might occur in any LMS must be considered and defined. In [40], a security attack is defined as an intentional act by which an entity attempts to evade security services and violate the security policy of a system. This definition is focused on violating the security services, it therefore considers security properties and attacks that could be classified according to each property. Another reason why we will adopt this properties-based model is that each property is connected to security PKI solutions, which can be applied to LMS. Both the properties-based model and the PKI solutions will be presented in this chapter.

2.2.2 SECURITY ATTACKS IN e-LEARNING

The lack of security in e-Learning is also supported by practical and real attacks in ICT. As a matter of fact, recent attack reports [4,5] have evidenced a significant number of real-life security attacks suffered by organizations and educational institutions. The is a cooperative survey research conducted by leading companies and educational institutions [4]. The report reveals that security attacks are a reality for most organizations: 81% of respondents' organizations experienced a security issue (ie, an adverse event that threatened some aspect of security).

Since LMS are software packages that integrate tools to support e-Learning activities, technological vulnerabilities have to be considered. Thus recent security reports [4,5] have shown how Web application servers and database management systems, which usually support LMS infrastructure, are deployed with security flaws. Dealing with more technological details related to LMSs, the Trustwave Global Security Report shows how Web application servers and database management systems are deployed with security vulnerabilities [5]. Moreover, potential LMS attacks can be studied by analyzing their specific security vulnerabilities. For instance, in Moodle Security Announcements [6], there were 49 serious vulnerabilities reported in 2013.

Regarding security in educational institutions in the scope of Spanish universities, the RedIRIS Computer Emergency Response Team is aimed at the early detection of security incidents affecting their affiliated institutions. As stated in [7], the total amount of incidents received in 2013 was 10,028, which represents an increase of 74.15% compared to the previous year. In the same context, in [8], the authors stated that only 17% of Spanish universities have adopted the application of the Spanish National Security Framework and only 18% of students use digital certificates.

In addition, these plans and initiatives are not related to security in e-Learning and pedagogical processes but to provide secure e-Administration and online management in virtual universities. In contrast, security in e-Learning processes is not usually considered. For instance, a student who is able to obtain a course certificate following advanced security techniques, such as a digital signature, may find the same security level is not required when performing e-Assessment activities.

Finally, from a broader perspective, the Global Risks Report [41] highlights how global risks are interconnected and have systemic impacts. To manage global risks effectively and build resilience to their impacts, better efforts are needed to understand, measure, and foresee the evolution of risks. According to Harris [41], the escalation in large-scale cyber attacks and the breakdown of critical information infrastructure are prominent risks. Furthermore, the technological risks of cyber attacks, data fraud, theft, and critical information infrastructure breakdown are strongly connected to each other and to other global risks—even global governance failure. This reflects the changing nature of security attacks and the need for global multidisciplinary collaboration to manage IS.

2.2.3 MODELING SECURITY SERVICES

Information security (IS) in ICT can be defined as a combination of properties that are provided by security services [42,43]. A basic security approach is the classic CIA triad that defines the three main targets of security services: confidentiality, integrity, and availability [42]. In addition, in [43] an extension to this model is proposed, including additional elements, such as possession or access control, authenticity, and utility. However, when considering technological factors other authors [44] explain that since software bugs are commonplace to software, it follows that security software could also have bugs. Finally, even though security properties defined in [43] could be taken as a first reference, it is necessary to offer additional facilities, such as audit service and failure control in order to reduce the effects and negative consequences of security vulnerabilities since the model proposed is not completely reliable.

Nowadays, ICT solutions based on PKI models are available to offer technological implementations of services that ensure the security issues that have been described and required in LMSs [45]. PKI, simply defined, is an infrastructure that allows for the creation of a trusted method for providing privacy, authentication, integrity, and nonrepudiation in communications between two parties. Since 1999, PKI related standards and specifications are available, such as the Internet X.509 public key infrastructure (PKIX) defined in [46] that was developed with the aim of building Internet standards to support a pervasive security infrastructure whose services are implemented and delivered using PKI techniques. As is the case elsewhere, there is no such thing as a free lunch in security services!

Finally, holistic approaches of IS need to be addressed [47] involving different areas, such as legal aspects and privacy legislation, secure software development, networking and secure protocols, ISMS, standards and methodologies, certification organizations, and security testing methods and tools. These approaches have introduced more complex security properties, such as authorship or nonrepudiation.

To sum up, IS can be defined as a combination of abstract security services or properties, based on the Request For Comments 4949, Internet Security Glossary, Version 2 [40], as follows:

- The classic CIA triad:
  - *Confidentiality*. The property that information is not made available or disclosed to unauthorized individuals, entities, or processes, that is, to any unauthorized entity of the information system.
  - *Integrity*. The property that data has not been changed, destroyed, or lost in an unauthorized or accidental manner.
  - *Availability*. The property of a system or a system resource being accessible and usable upon demand by an authorized system entity, according to performance specifications for the system. In other words, a system is available if it provides services according to the system design whenever users request them.
- Parker-enhanced properties:
  - *Access control*. Protection of system resources against unauthorized access. The use of system resources is regulated according to a security policy and is permitted by only authorized entities.
  - *Identity*. An act or process that presents an identifier to a system so that the system can recognize a system entity and distinguish it from other entities.
  - *Authentication* (closely related to identity). The process of verifying an identity claimed by or for a system entity.
- Additional PKI properties:
  - *Time stamping*. With respect to a data object, a label or mark in which the time when the label or mark was affixed to the data object is recorded.
  - *Nonrepudiation*. A security service that provides protection against false denial of involvement in a communication process or, in general, regarding the actions of system entities.
- Considering full security does not exist:
  - *Audit*. A security service that records information needed to establish accountability for system events and for the actions of system entities that cause them.
  - *Failure control*. A methodology used to provide fail-safe or fail-soft termination and recovery of functions and processes when failures are detected or occur in a system.

Following this approach, which is based on abstract security properties, we define IS as the condition of a system that results from the establishment and maintenance of the following properties: availability, integrity, confidentiality, access control, identity, authentication, time stamping, nonrepudiation, audit, and failure control.

2.2.4 **SECURITY IN e-LEARNING: REAL e-LEARNING SCENARIOS**

In this section, we illustrate the previous security attacks and models in e-Learning based on a real case study.

The case study focuses on aspects that may occur in e-Learning scenarios aimed at discovering essential factors in secure e-Learning. Although this example can be seen as a hypothetical case, it has been motivated by the UOC collaborative learning model and a real activity developed in the UOC Doctoral Programme in Education and ICT. A short summary of this activity is included below:

- *Participants*: A group of PhD candidates and the tutor.
- *Main goal*: To discover how their research topics are related to security in e-Learning.
- *LMS tools*: Every e-Learning tool is integrated in a Moodle LMS.
- *Stages of the activity and LMS tools*:
  - *Task 1*: Assignments and outcomes tool. Students introduce their research topics in relation to IS and they submit a static document.
  - *Task 2*: Content Management System. The tutor reviews individual work, makes suggestions (which could introduce changes), and the result is published.
  - *Task 3*: Forum module. Students carry out open discussions.
  - *Task 4*: Wiki/collaborative document. Participants develop a collaborative document collecting common relations.

As stated by Laforcade [48] educational modeling languages aim, in essence, to describe the content and process in order to support reuse and interoperability. In order to integrate educational modeling with security analysis we use unified modeling language (UML) as UML diagrams can provide an overview of layered security, and they are easy to understand [49]. From this view, we can analyze security requirements in our case study by UML diagrams.

The component diagram (Fig. 2.1) shows the case components, their relations, and the following attacks (attackers are represented as black figures):

1. *Virus attack*: The LMS contains a virus file, which is downloaded and run at start up of students' devices and operating systems, to cause malicious effects.
2. *Denial of service*: An external agent makes the LMS unavailable to its authorized users.
3. *Sniffing network*: A student is able to listen to private and unauthorized communications or sniffing other users' credentials.
4. *Denial of involvement*: A student could submit a post to a discussion forum, and then claim that he did not submit the post.
5. *Domain name system (DNS) or Web spoofing*: Students are directed to a website that looks like the LMS they believe they are visiting.
6. *Man-in-the-middle attack*: The server itself may be supplanted by an external agent using a man-in-the-middle attack.
7. *Credential spoofing*: A student presents a convincing false identity to others.

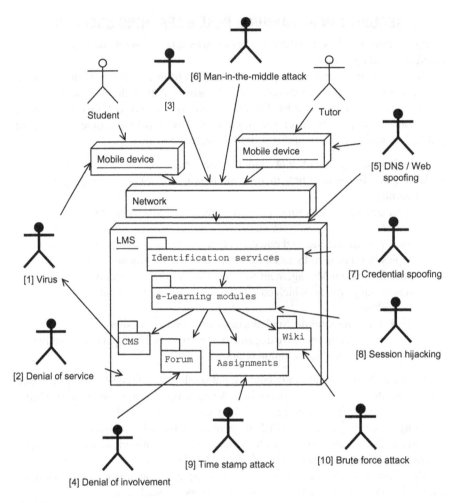

FIG. 2.1

Component diagram modeling vulnerabilities.

8. *Session hijacking*: A students' personal data is accessed by an unauthorized entity.
9. *Time stamp attack*: The time stamp of assignments that have been submitted is altered.
10. *Brute force attack*: Wiki pages are altered through running automated scripts.

Moreover, we can describe the student's total activity through a diagram or workflow. For this purpose a *sequence diagram* (see Fig. 2.2) models an ordinary scenario including an attack combining different actions and techniques. This example also illustrates the security properties that are mainly violated in each action.

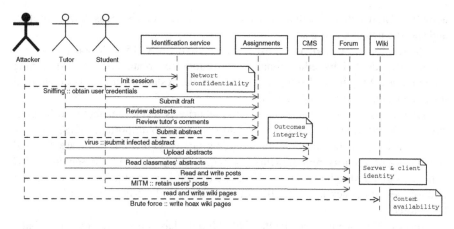

FIG. 2.2

Sequence diagram modeling attack actions and properties.

In the sequence diagram describing the attacker's actions (see Fig. 2.2) some labels representing information system elements are included as well as security properties of these elements that have been violated due to an attacker's action. As presented in previous sections, we propose an abstract model focused on how each type of attack would violate the security services. For instance, if an attacker is able to read and write forum posts in an unauthorized manner by using fake credentials, the agent (a student in the information system) has not been properly identified, that is, the identity property has not been fulfilled. Therefore this learning activity is not secure.

2.3 SECURE LEARNING MANAGEMENT SYSTEMS

Coordination, collaboration, and communication processes for e-Learning, as well as management learning activities, should be supported in an integrated management system. According to Flate [50], an LMS is a broad term that is used for a wide range of systems that organize and provide access to e-Learning services to students, teachers, and administrators. These services usually include access control, provision of learning content, communication tools, and organizations of user groups [51]. In this sense, LMSs are software packages that enable the management of educational content and also integrate tools to support most collaboration needs, such as e-mail, discussion forums, instant messaging (chat), virtual classrooms, and so on [51].

Over recent years, a great number of full-featured Web-based LMS systems have appeared in the marketplace, offering designers and instructors generic, powerful, user-friendly layouts for the easy and rapid creation and organization of courses and activities. These activities can then be customized to the tutor's needs, learner profile, and specific pedagogical goals [51].

Moodle [52] is one of the most representative LMSs [53]. Moodle has been extensively adopted by educational organizations to create effective e-Learning communities. They have also highly customized the system to suit their pedagogical needs and technological requirements.

Since LMSs are software components, security is a relevant factor to be considered. Despite the great support of LMS systems to important areas, such as communication, collaboration, and coordination, very few of them are focused specifically on security requirements [54–56]. Namely, the study presented in [54] concludes that a Moodle server is vulnerable to well-known attacks, such as session fixation, session hijacking, prediction of user names and prediction of passwords by brute force.

According to Kumar and Dutta [56], Moodle has much vulnerability related to authentication, availability, confidentiality, and integrity attacks. Therefore it is necessary to develop a mechanism that defends these security flaws. The authors present the most common security flaws and suggest the optimal security settings of Moodle.

We can tackle the development of secure LMS with PKI solutions. In [55], a registration protocol that allows the incorporation of a PKI infrastructure into a Moodle e-Learning environment was designed. This model makes it possible to endow the system with all the features supported by public key cryptography. This security enhancement means a step toward a more robust, private, and secure system.

2.4 SECURITY FOR e-LEARNING PARADIGMS

Next we briefly review popular learning paradigms and methodologies involved in our research for secure e-Learning. At the end, we delimit the scope of the book.

2.4.1 COLLABORATIVE LEARNING

Over the past decade, CSCL has become one of the most influential learning paradigms devoted to improving teaching and learning with the help of modern information and communication technology [1].

Computer-supported collaborative learning (CSCL) also refers to instructional methods where students are encouraged to work together on learning tasks. As an example, project-based learning (PBL) has proved to be a very successful method to that end. Therefore CSCL applications aim to create virtual collaborative learning environments where students, teachers, and tutors are able to cooperate with each other in order to accomplish a common learning goal [14].

To achieve common learning goals, CSCL applications provide support to three essential aspects of collaboration, namely coordination, collaboration, and communication [57]. Communication is the basis for achieving coordination and collaboration. Collaboration and communication might be synchronous or asynchronous. The former means cooperation at the same time where the shared resource will not typically have a lifespan beyond the sharing. The latter means cooperation at different times with the shared resource stored in a persistent support.

The representation and analysis of group activity interaction is an important issue in CSCL for the support of coaching and evaluation in online collaborative learning environments [1]. Interaction analysis relies on information captured from the actions performed by the participants during the collaborative process. To this end, fine-grained notifications and complex information collected from the interactions of learners are provided to give immediate feedback about the activities of others and about the collaboration in general [58].

The study of security for CSCL requires the identification of certain functionalities related to the specific context and characteristics of the CSCL. Some main representative CSCL features presented in this section can be summarized in the following list:

1. *Interactions among participants*: CSCL usually demands a great number of communication processes and different types of interactions.
2. *Groupwork*: When the knowledge is produced and transmitted collaboratively, the learning framework is usually managed by defining work groups.
3. *Generation of collaborative results*: Collaborative contents management systems are required in order to manage collaborative knowledge.
4. *Communication processes*: Communication is the basis for achieving coordination and collaboration.

A common limitation when moving from e-Learning to CSCL settings is that collaborative learning is seen as another feature of the LMS and the security requirements do not consider any specific requirements for CSCL. For instance, identification of e-Learning criteria has been discussed in detail in [59] from the disciplines of educational science, software engineering, or technological security. For each discipline, specific requirements are defined and CSCL is only included as an educational aspect (social support by collaboration and communication). Therefore CSCL design needs a revision in order to support specific security needs.

2.4.2 MOBILE LEARNING

Mobile learning (ML) has emerged lately with the ever increasing use of mobile technology in education. According to Luo and Zhang [60] and Caballé et al. [61] the needs of educational organizations are increasingly more related to modern e-Learning environments. These environments must provide advanced capability for the distribution of learning activities and the necessary features and learning resources to all participants, regardless of where these participants and resources are located, and whether this location is static or dynamic. The aim of the new generation of learning systems is to enable the learning experience in open, dynamic, large-scale, and heterogeneous environments through smart mobile devices. According to Sharples et al. [62], mobile learning requires a reconceptualization of the learning model in order to recognize the essential role of mobility and communication in e-Learning, to indicate the importance of context in establishing meaning, and to specify the effect of digital networks in supporting virtual communities.

According to Caballé et al. [61], mobile technologies will become more ubiquitous, pervasive, and networked, with enhanced capabilities for rich social interactions, context awareness, and Internet connectivity. Such technologies can have a great impact on collaborative learning. Learning will move increasingly outside the formal classroom and into the learner's own environments, both physical and virtual, thus becoming more situated, personal, collaborative, and informal.

Although, from a general point of view, ML can be considered as anytime and anywhere learning experiences, the authors in [63] showed how we can consider multiple definitions of m-Learning. Moreover, because of the complexity and multidisciplinary factors of the mobile computer-supported collaborative learning (MCSCL) paradigm, in [61] a three-dimensional approach has been provided to understand and unify the dispersion currently existing in advanced learning practices and pedagogical goals from the era of Mobile MCSCL. This approach considers the context of MCSCL from a multidimensional perspective: pedagogical, technological and evaluative.

In this book we will focus ML especially on the use of mobile devices (ie, tablets and smart phones) when developing CSCL activities. In this sense, ML educational process can be considered as any learning and teaching activity that is possible through mobile tools or in settings where mobile equipment is available [63].

Regarding mobile technologies, mobile devices are closely related to wireless networks and Web services; therefore, the attacks presented previously in the LMS context should also be considered in mobile collaborative learning. According to Sathyan and Sadasivan [64], there are specific ML threats in the collaborative approaches on ensuring mobile applications and devices: blue bugging, blue jacking, blue snarfing, device cloning, eavesdropping, falsification of content, cryptanalytic, and man-in-the-middle. among them, the first three categories are actually specific for MCSCL because they are connected to built-in mobile components and services. Although the other threats are also applicable to standard devices, this classification presents the current most significant risks in mobile devices.

2.4.3 MASSIVE OPEN ONLINE COURSES

Over the last few years we have witnessed the hype of massive open online courses (MOOCs). MOOCs are defined as open, free, participatory, and distributed courses that represent a new generation of online education, are easily and widely accessible on the Internet, and involve a large or very large number of students [65]. Although the term MOOC was first used in 2008 by Dave Cormier and Bryan Alexander [66], we can find pioneered initiatives such as OpenCourseWare in 2002 [67].

The MOOC concept has its origin in an open class offered by George Siemens in 2008 [68]. Siemens developed an e-Learning website and, in 2002, he started publishing a weekly newsletter on education, technology, and knowledge trends. In this context, he started to look at how openness of content and social interactions could change; however, the low levels of adoption in Web 2.0 and social media made it difficult to accomplish the vision of scaling the number of participants. From this incipient learning experience, in 2008, Siemens proposed a more advanced learning initiative based on:

- high levels of learner interaction control;
- synchronous sessions with facilitators and guest speakers;
- frequent newsletters as regular contact points for course participants;
- tracking services for blogs of course participants;
- increasing learner autonomy in selecting learning resources and activities;
- maximizing the use of social systems as effective means for learners to self-organize their learning process;
- emphasis on the learner's understanding of the course topics through blogs, concept maps, videos, images, and podcasts.

The participation levels and academic results of this open course demonstrated the success of the first MOOC developed by Siemens and his team.

More recently, in [69], the most significant MOOC experiences are presented and the term MOOC is defined as:

1. *Open*: The participants can read and comment on the course.
2. *Free*: The participants can take the MOOC without paying.
3. *Shared*: The work and information in the course is shared with all the participants.
4. *Participatory*: The participants gain knowledge by engaging with other people's work.
5. *Distributed*: The collaborative and networking activities are part of the MOOC; however, they do not need to reside on the same platform.

Although current top-ranked academic communities have already joined the MOOC hype, other academic sectors hold controversial discussions on MOOC challenges that must be faced before moving forward [65] to put them into learning practice. Issues such as high drop-out rates, poor grading, plagiarism and security vulnerabilities, such as anomalous authentication. Indeed, while MOOCs are easily and widely accessible, and as such typically succeed in involving a very large number of participants, anomalous user authentication cannot ensure that the actual identity of the MOOC students is actually known in order to verify whether MOOC students are who they say they are or are instead cheating the system [70].

Current deliverers of MOOCs are very concerned about this user authentication issue and make great efforts to know and verify student identity during the MOOC sessions. For instance, they use biometrics (eg, typing patterns) and other complicated mechanisms, which sometimes prove to be unreliable and are often privacy intrusive [71]. This also becomes a particular issue for satisfying accrediting institutions and hiring companies that rely on the emergent MOOC educational phenomenon [70,72].

Innovative user authentication methods for verifying MOOC student identity are required, so that the course progress and results are not compromised by either incompetence or malice [73]. Providing security approaches specifically to MOOC, and in particular effective student authentication (ie, ensuring that students are who they say they are), has been claimed by some authors as an essential feature in the MOOC arena, especially for evaluation, grading, and eventual certification purposes [71,74]. For instance, course certification can make all the difference for business models based on value-added services of MOOC that require the identity of the student to be actually known and verified [70]. Recently, some popular MOOC platforms, such as Coursera [71], have developed complex mechanisms based on keystroke biometrics (eg, typing patterns) to verify the identity of participants during MOOC sessions. However, biometric methods are still unreliable and privacy intrusive [75].

2.5 DISCUSSION

CSCL activities usually involve various use cases, actors, processes, requirements, and learning objectives in the complex context of e-Learning [14]. To address this complexity we limit the scope of the book to the most commonplace CSCL activities, namely, online collaborative assessment (also referred to as *collaborative e-Assessment*). In higher education e-Assessment is typically employed to deliver formative tests to the students and very little attention has been given to providing solutions to the unethical conduct of students such as cheating during e-Exams [16].

Regarding security in e-Assessment, in [16] the authors discussed how unethical conduct while taking an online exam may occur by circumventing agreed rules or gaining unfair advantages.

From the general perspective of e-Assessment, in this book, we particularize the general perspective to the online evaluation model used in the Open University of Catalonia (UOC) [76]. According to Sangrà [77], evaluation models used at UOC may be classified in accordance with the following factors or dimensions:

1. *Subject type*: The type of subject is determined by several factors, such as the educational model or the number of students (eg, a collaborative subject following an intensive collaborative learning model and performed by few students arranged in learning groups).
2. *Evaluation and grading model*: The UOC evaluation model is devoted to assisting students in achieving their learning objectives. The university employs a continuous assessment (CA) evaluation system during each semester. This evaluation is optional, as all students must still sit for their final exam. To

achieve balance, course results are weighted between the assessment of the entire course and final exam results.

3. *Evaluation application*: This dimension considers manual (ie, tutors participate directly and intensely in the evaluation process) and automatic (minimal participation) applications.
4. *Agents involved in the evaluation processes*: We can consider both participants and services, for instance, students carrying out learning activities in a LMS who are assessed by tutors.

Our assessment model is a P2P e-Assessment model, namely, a model where students mutually evaluate peer activities and contributions during the learning process, such as in a network. Our P2P assessment model is aligned with recent collaborative models based on collective intelligence, P2P assessment, and social networks. According to Mazzara et al. [78] collective intelligence is a group or shared intelligence that emerges from the collaboration and or competition of many entities. Previous research on collective intelligence [78–80] demonstrates how the resulting information generated by collaborative models can be seen as reflecting the collective knowledge of a community of users and can be used for different purposes.

Trustworthiness for secure collaborative learning

3.1 BACKGROUND

In this section, we provide an overview of the main concepts, methods, and techniques found in the literature on the use of trustworthiness for e-Learning.

3.1.1 GENERAL TRUSTWORTHINESS MODELS

According to Gambetta [81], there is a degree of convergence on the definition of trustworthiness. This can be summarized as follows: trustworthiness is a particular level of the subjective probability with which an agent assesses another agent (or group of agents) performing a particular action, before the agent can monitor such action (or independently of his capacity ever to be able to monitor it) and in a context in which it affects the agent's own action.

As stated by Raza et al. [82] through the study of the most relevant existing trust models, trustworthiness modeling can be classified into trustworthiness evaluation and prediction models (literature on trustworthiness modeling also uses the terms "determination" and "estimation" to refer to "assessment" and "prediction," respectively). The first formal trustworthiness model related to information technology (IT) services was proposed in [10] from three levels. This approach considers the main factors and rules dealing with trustworthiness, which can be summarized as follows:

1. *Basic trust*: The general trusting disposition of an agent at a certain point in time.
2. *General trust*: The trust that an agent has in another agent at a certain point in time.
3. *Situational trust*: The amount of trust taking into account a specific situation.

Software components related to trustworthiness modules have been developed recently, such as FeelTrust [13], which is an application for smart-phones that automatically monitors the overall trustworthiness levels of users. FeelTrust classifies users the trustworthiness of users depending on their interests. It pairs this result with feedback from an embedded reputation system. As stated by the authors,

Intelligent Data Analysis for e-Learning. http://dx.doi.org/10.1016/B978-0-12-804535-0.00003-4

the FeelTrust implementation demonstrates the feasibility of security tasks using trustworthiness models. This approach is based on two modules oriented to collect trustworthiness data: Monitor Behavior that monitors and collects sensor data and Manage Feedback that manages feedback (ie, scores, ratings or recommendations).

A resource description framework (RDF) [83] is a standard model for data interchange on the Web. In [84] the authors proposed a trust model for RDF data that considers trustworthiness on the level of data sources. This model is devoted to enabling a trust infrastructure for the Web by developing concepts for automatic trust assessment based on provenance information and on the opinion of other information users. Furthermore, this approach provides trust-aware data access methods and concepts to implement trust-aware systems.

3.1.2 TRUSTWORTHINESS FACTORS AND RULES

With the purpose of measuring and modeling trustworthiness, in [85] the authors designed a survey to explore interpersonal trust in work groups, identifying trust-building behaviors ranked in order of importance. These behaviors can be classified into trustworthiness building factor (TBF) and trustworthiness reducing factor (TRF) as trustworthiness factors to measure general trust.

The factors for modeling trustworthiness when students are performing collaborative activities are summarized in Table 3.1.

Table 3.1 Trustworthiness Building and Reducing Factors

No.	Factors and Description
	Trustworthiness building factor (TBF) Student *S* working in the group of students *GS* is building trustworthiness when...
1	*S* communicates honestly, without distorting any information
2	*S* shows confidence in GSs abilities
3	*S* keeps promises and commitments
4	*S* listens to and values what GS say, even though *S* might not agree
5	*S* cooperates with GS and looks for mutual help
	Trustworthiness reducing factor (TRF) Student *S* working in the group of students *GS* is reducing trustworthiness when...
1	*S* acts more concerned about own welfare than anything else
2	*S* sends mixed messages so that GS never know where *S* stands
3	*S* avoids taking responsibility
4	*S* jumps to conclusions without checking the facts first
5	*S* makes excuses or blames others when things do not work out

Moreover, according to Liu and Wu [86], there are different aspects when considering trust as well as different expressions and classifications of trust issues. In essence, we summarize these aspects by defining the following rules:

1. *Asymmetry*: *A* trusts *B* is not equal to *B* trusts *A*.
2. *Time factor*: Trustworthiness is dynamic and may evolve over time.
3. *Limited transitivity*: If *A* trusts *C* who trusts *B* then *A* will also trust *B*, but while the process goes on, trust will not be absolutely reliable.
4. *Context sensitive*: When context changes, trust relationship might change too.

In [85] the authors proposed a data provenance trust model, which takes into account various factors that may affect trustworthiness. Based on these factors, the model assigns trust scores to both data and data providers. These scores represent key information and users that may decide whether to use the data and for what purposes. The trust score of an item is computed by taking into account four factors:

1. *Data similarity*: The likeness of different scores in the same set.
2. *Path similarity*: The intermediate agents that processed data from source to destination.
3. *Data conflict*: Inconsistent descriptions or information about the same entity.
4. *Data deduction*: If the source information or the responsible party is highly trusted, the resulting data will also be highly trusted.

To sum up, trustworthiness components, features, and factors identified in these sections about trustworthiness models [87–89] are summarized in Fig. 3.1.

3.1.3 TRUSTWORTHINESS IN e-LEARNING

According to Liu and Wu [86], a Trustworthy LMS is an e-Learning system that contains reliable peer services and useful learning resources.

Among functional approaches, trustworthiness analysis, modeling, assessment, and prediction methods are suitable in the context of CSCL [89,90]. Trustworthiness can be considered as a suitable functional factor in CSCL because most trustworthiness models are based on P2P interactions [10,11] and CSCL is closely related to student-to-student interactions. Although some trustworthiness methods have been proposed and investigated, they have been little investigated in CSCL with the aim of enhancing security properties. Therefore, we propose to conduct research on security in CSCL by enhancing technological security solutions with trustworthiness, and through experimenting with methods, techniques, and trustworthiness models. We will eventually arranged trustworthiness methodology approach for collaborative e-Learning [87].

In [60] the authors presented a service platform for e-Learning with trustworthy service provisioning. This service is based on an integration of grid services, on demand e-Learning, and trusted assets tracking. The service platform, called MiQ-SP [60], is designed for e-Learning with trustworthy service provisioning; it is

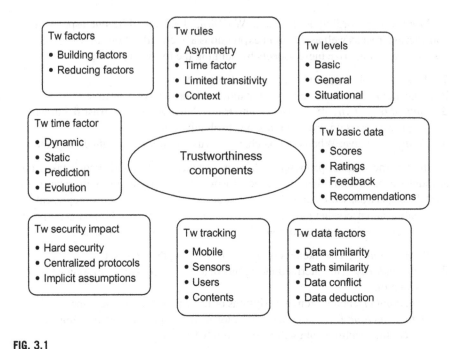

FIG. 3.1

Trustworthiness components, features, and factors. *Tw*, trustworthiness.

developed based on an integrated service network concept for tracking e-Learning participants and managing e-Learning assets.

The studies presented in [91,92] stem from the difficulties of guaranteeing the quality and trustworthiness of learning resources and participants. These drawbacks cause learners and educators to have insufficient confidence to participate in Web-based learning [91] and it may sometimes be difficult for users to select the most appropriate content themselves, in order to enhance their learning experience [92]. To this end, in [91] the authors proposed a quality assured and trustworthy e-Learning environment with quality certification and trust evaluation. This model is based on a service-oriented architecture and combines static quality certification and dynamic trust evaluation. The trustworthiness approach presented in [92] is based on trustworthiness, similarity, and knowledge gains. As stated by the authors, this model provides an effective solution to support peer-based information sharing within Web-based contexts.

In [93] the authors presented a P2P based social network to enhance the quality of e-Learning. This network is based on knowledge sharing in virtual learning communities. In order to organize and provide better resource management, each peer has to classify content and evaluate its quality (ie, rating of the resource), the number of times the site is accessed, and the matching degree by which the content classification conforms to the knowledge domain [93].

3.1.4 NORMALIZED TRUSTWORTHINESS MODELS

Although trustworthiness models can be defined and included as a service in e-Learning security frameworks, there are multiple issues related to trustworthiness that cannot be managed without normalization [94], such as trustworthiness multiple sources, different data formats, measuring techniques, and other trustworthiness issues (eg, rules, evolution, or context).

The concept of normalized trustworthiness is introduced in [94] as a trust relationship in terms of a vector, which is normalized by a trust policy. Each element in a trust vector represents a parameter that contributes toward the trust evaluation in a specific time and context (ie, A trusts B at a time T and for a particular context C). The normalization model is based on the trust policy vector, which is a vector that has the same dimension as the trust vector. The elements are real numbers in the range $[0, 1]$ and the sum of all elements is equal to 1. Hence, each normalized value is the result of a trustworthiness value multiplied by the corresponding weight in the policy vector.

Later works [95–97] improved the normalization process by proposing more complex functions. As stated in [95], a simple arithmetic average would perform a rough compensation between high and low trustworthiness values. In order to address this drawback, the authors proposed the weighted ordered weighted averaging (WOWA), which uses two sets of weights: one corresponds to the relevance of the sources, and the other corresponds to the relevance of the trustworthiness values. According to Li et al. [97] a lightweight mathematical model can be used to represent the collected evidence. Following this model, all the trustworthy evidence is represented as a vector and then the trustworthy values can be represented as a trustworthy matrix where each row of the matrix is a trustworthiness item, and each column is a trustworthiness value. Moreover, the preferences of trustworthy evidence are represented as a weight vector. After normalization, the trustworthiness of each user can be evaluated as the normalized matrix (ie, multiplication between a trustworthiness matrix and a weight vector).

Another perspective is focused on normalizing trustworthiness values by subtracting the average value for a user. In [98] the authors introduced the concept of the filler mean target difference attribute as the overall average subtracted from a specific rating as a normalizing factor. This technique is also proposed in [96] with the aim of normalizing the vectors representing the profiles of items by the utility value. Finally, in [99] the authors presented how to estimate information trustworthiness by considering multiple information sources. This problem is formulated as a joint matrix factorization procedure where different sets of users from different sources are partitioned into common groups and rating behavior of groups is assumed to be consistent across sources.

3.1.5 **TIME FACTOR AND TRUSTWORTHINESS SEQUENCES**

Several studies investigating trustworthiness show that *time factor* is strongly related to trustworthiness [86,100,101]. The authors in [86] stated that trust is dynamic and will attenuate when time goes by. For instance, A trusts B at time t_0, but A might not trust B in a follow-up time t_1. In [94] the authors presented the design and development of a trust management system. This system addresses its specifications and architecture to facilitate the system implementation through a module-oriented architecture. Among the modules of the system, the authors define a module for dynamic assessment, which includes trust level assessment based on dynamic trust criteria. The module integrates assessment from all parts to calculate trust value by the weighted average.

Furthermore, we can consider both assessment and prediction trustworthiness models. Although the models reviewed for analyzing trustworthiness include time factor as a key component, we need further modeling techniques that allow for steering trustworthiness evaluation toward prediction. To this end, the concept of Trustworthiness History Sequence is relevant [101]. In the context of grid services, Trustworthiness History Sequence is a historical record of the trustworthiness of grid services with which the requester has traded. It can be denoted with an ordered tuple where each component is the trustworthiness score of the transaction between a requester and a service.

3.1.6 **PREDICTING TRUSTWORTHINESS**

Trustworthiness prediction models have also been little investigated in the context of e-Learning, CSCL, and e-Assessment activities, even in a general prediction scope. The existing literature suggests that the term trust prediction is used equivalently and interchangeably with the trust assessment process [82]. Moreover, trustworthiness does not focus on an isolated technical application, but on the social context in which it is embedded. Although trustworthiness building can be supported by institutions, there is no easy solution [102]. In addition, the building of trust can be a very long process, the outcome of which is very hard to predict.

Several studies [82,101,103] investigating trustworthiness prediction were carried out with neural network (NN) as one of the most reliable methods for predicting values. The authors in [82] proposed the use of neural networks to predict the trust values for any given entities. A neural network can capture any type of nonlinear relationship between input and output data through iterative training, which produces better prediction accuracy in any domain, such as time series prediction. The key contribution of this work is focused on the dynamic nature of trust, in which the performance of this approach is tested under four different types of data sets (eg, nonuniform stationary data, different size, etc.), and the optimal configuration of the neural network is identified.

The authors in [101] stated that trustworthiness prediction with the method of NN is feasible. The experiments presented in [101] confirmed that the methods with NNs are effective for predicting trustworthiness. This method was based on defining a NN structure, an input standardization, a training sample construction, and the procedure of predicting trustworthiness with a trained neural network.

The work presented in [103] proposed a novel application of NNs in evaluating multiple recommendations of various trust standards. This contribution presents the design of a trust model to derive recommendation trust from heterogeneous agents. The experimental results show that the model has robust performance when there are high prediction accuracy requirements or when there are deceptive recommendations.

Moreover, other prediction trustworthiness models were proposed without NN methods, such as similarity approaches [104,105]. The authors in [105] stated that predicting trust among the agents is of great importance to various open distributed settings. The author focuses the study on P2P systems in which dishonest agents can easily join the system and achieve their goals by circumventing agreed rules or gaining unfair advantages. These cases are closely related to e-Assessment regarding anomalous assessment processes as well as integrity and identity security properties. To this end, this work proposed a trust prediction approach to capture dynamic behavior of the target agent by identifying features, which are capable of describing the context of a transaction.

A further work on user rating systems [104] presented experimental results which demonstrated that the number of ratings is positively associated with trust, as well as the congruence between one's own opinion and the opinion of others. This study also demonstrated that rating source and volume have an impact on credibility perceptions, reliance on user-generated information, and opinion congruence. These results indicate important theoretical extensions by demonstrating that social information may be filtered through signals indicating its veracity, which may not apply equally to all social users.

3.1.7 RELATED TRUSTWORTHINESS METHODOLOGICAL APPROACHES

As previously mentioned, little research has been carried out to build trustworthiness methodological approaches. In the context of business processes, in [106] the authors proposed a generic methodology, called trustworthiness measurement methodology. This methodology can be used to determine both the quality of service of a given provider and the quality of product. The scope of this study is the business processes, but the key concept of this methodology is the interaction between agents. This topic can be seen as quite close to collaborative learning, just considering student interactions and trustworthiness between them. This methodology is based on the following phases:

1. determining the context of interaction between the trusting agent and the trusted entity;
2. determining the criteria involved in the interaction;

3. developing a criterion assessment policy for each criterion involved in the interaction; and
4. determining the trustworthiness value of the trusted entity in the given context.

The authors in [107] presented the foundations of formal models for trust in global IS environments with the aim of underpinning the use of trustworthiness based security mechanisms as an alternative to the traditional ones. As stated by the authors, this formal model is based on a novel notion of trust structures that are built on concepts from trust management and domain theory. The formal model is focused on the following target principles:

1. Trustworthiness involves entities.
2. Trustworthiness has a degree.
3. Trustworthiness is based on observations.
4. Trustworthiness determines the interaction among entities.

In addition to the methodology and formal approaches, a trust architecture by introducing a basic trust management model was presented in [108].

3.2 KNOWLEDGE MANAGEMENT FOR TRUSTWORTHINESS e-LEARNING DATA

In this section we propose consideration of a knowledge management (KM) process to support collaborative learning. In particular, a KM process for managing trustworthy data in e-Learning is proposed later in Chapter 5 with the aim of enhancing security in CSCL and in particular in e-Learning teams.

Our KM process is based on previous data management approaches [109].

Throughout this section, we present the necessary background for our security approach in the CSCL context. Furthermore, data visualization of trustworthy data from general e-Learning systems is commonplace in data analysis as a means to facilitate reading and understanding of the results extracted from the data.

Therefore the main goal of this section is to analyze existing data management approaches to support trustworthiness data by a suitable set of KM techniques and models. Finally, data visualization and knowledge discovery tools are included in our approach to allow e-Learning stakeholders to manage security, such as anomalous student behavior in online group activities.

3.2.1 KNOWLEDGE MANAGEMENT PROCESS

As a key process in higher education, KM aims at capturing explicit and tacit knowledge in order to facilitate the access, sharing, and reuse of that knowledge as well as to create new knowledge and facilitate organizational learning. To succeed, KM must be guided by a strategic vision to fulfill primary organizational objectives [110], such as improving knowledge sharing and cooperative work, disseminating best practices, improving relationships with the external world, and preserving past knowledge for reuse [111]. In this sense, in [109] the authors faced the challenge of extracting the relevant knowledge to provide learners and tutors with efficient awareness, feedback, and monitoring support in CSCL. To this end, they propose a conceptual model for KM that identifies and classifies the many kinds of indicators that describe collaboration and learning in CSCL.

Therefore in this chapter we discuss issues related to standardizing the management of trustworthiness information and knowledge extraction in CSCL for security purposes by following existing KM processes and methods, and also from experience. In particular, we follow the interaction data analysis process described in [109] for transforming information generated from different sources of CSCL activities into useful knowledge in an efficient manner for individual and group awareness, feedback, monitoring, and scaffolding. The corresponding knowledge discovery process for CSCL proposed by these authors [109,112] drives the KM enhancements proposed in this chapter. As a result, in order to provide adequate support to the management of trustworthiness data from CSCL activities, four separate, steps are necessary: collection of information, processing, analysis, and presentation (see Fig. 3.2). This figure shows how the quantitative information collected in the form of events is first classified and structured. As can be seen in Fig. 3.2, the information is then analyzed in order to extract the desired knowledge. The final step is to provide users with the essential awareness and feedback from the obtained knowledge. The entire process would fail if any one of these steps is omitted [109]:

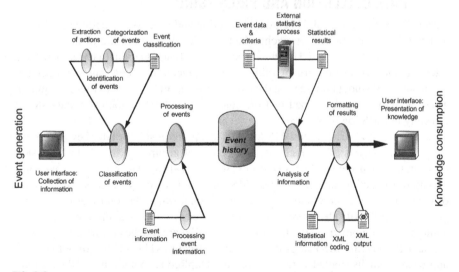

FIG. 3.2

The process of transforming event information into knowledge in CSCL [109].

1. *Data collection*: To collect all the necessary data produced from the CSCL activities in an efficient manner.
2. *Data processing*: Classification of the collected data and processing in a suitable data structure for later analysis.
3. *Analysis*: Structured data is then analyzed in order to extract the desired knowledge.
4. *Presentation*: To provide users with the awareness and feedback from the obtained knowledge.

In the context of CSCL, e-Assessment activities are characterized by a high degree of user-user and user-system interaction and hence they generate a huge amount of event information [112]. The student events data management involves three main design decisions:

1. How to obtain and classify the necessary data gathered from the CSCL activity.
2. How to efficiently process the large amount of information collected during the CSCL activity in order to facilitate its later analysis.
3. How information should be analyzed and what kind of knowledge should be extracted and presented to the actors of the learning process.

Although we take as our main reference the KM process for CSCL proposed in [109], the four general phases of this process presented next are extended by reviewing complementary research work related to each phase (note that the data collection and processing phases are reviewed together).

3.2.2 DATA COLLECTION AND PROCESSING

According to Caballé et al. [112], data collection and processing require an efficient and robust computational approach, which enables the embedding of the collected information and the extracted knowledge into a CSCL application. In order to provide effective and just-in-time trustworthiness data collection, a continuous processing and analysis of student interaction data during long term CSCL activities is required. These activities are developed in LMS and produce huge amounts of data stored typically in LMS log files [113].

Extracting and structuring LMS log data is a prerequisite for later key processes, such as the analysis of interactions, assessment of group activity, or the provision of awareness and feedback involved in CSCL [114–116]. The computational complexity of extracting and structuring LMS log files is a costly process. The amount of data tends to be large and needs computational power beyond that of a single processor [114,116]. Therefore to overcome these computational limitations, several authors have demonstrated the feasibility of parallel approaches for processing large log data files in real LMS using distributed infrastructures [113–116]. Among parallel approaches and distributed infrastructures, the MapReduce paradigm and the Hadoop framework [117] have become one of the most reliable and scalable computing approaches for massive data processing [113].

MapReduce is a programming model and an associated implementation for processing large data sets [118]. Users specify a *Map* function that processes a key/value pair to generate a set of intermediate key/value pairs, and a *Reduce* function that merges all intermediate values associated with the same intermediate key. In [113] the authors proposed the MapReduce paradigm as a suitable solution for the log file analysis. In this application, MapReduce workers are assigned to *Map* and *Reduce* tasks. Workers do parallel computation of *Map* tasks. So it does analysis of log files in just two phases *Map* and *Reduce* wherein the *Map* tasks generate intermediate results (key, value) pairs and the task provides the summarized value for a particular key.

The Apache Hadoop software library is a framework that provides the distributed processing of large data sets across clusters of computers using simple programming models. Hadoop is designed to scale up from single servers to thousands of machines, each offering local computation and storage [119]. This framework is best known for its MapReduce implementation and its distributed file system. The Hadoop MapReduce job is defined as a unit of work that the client wants to be performed consisting of the input data, MapReduce program, and configuration information. Then, Hadoop runs the job by dividing it into tasks of two types: *Map* and *Reduce* tasks. There are also two types of nodes: *tracker* that coordinates the parallel process and *workers* that perform the target job [119].

3.2.3 EDUCATIONAL DATA MINING AND LEARNING ANALYTICS

Regarding data analysis in e-Learning, two related research communities exist, educational data mining (EDM) and learning analytics (LA), also known as learning analytics and knowledge. While LA and EDM share many attributes and have similar goals and interests, they have some differences in technological, ideological, and methodological orientations [120].

A significant analysis and discussion of EDM was presented in [121]. In this study, the authors discussed how applying EDM is an emerging interdisciplinary research field that is concerned with developing methods for exploring the unique types of data that come from educational environments. According to Romero [122], on one hand, EDM is concerned with developing, researching, and applying computerized methods to detect patterns in large collections of educational data that would otherwise be hard or impossible to analyze due to the enormous volume of data within which they exist. On the other hand, LA is concerned with the measurement, collection, analysis, and reporting of data about learners and their contexts for the purposes of understanding and optimizing learning and the environments in which it occurs. For our purpose of discovering patterns of anomalous behavior during e-Learning activities, we take the EDM approach.

The majority of traditional data mining techniques, including but not limited to classification, clustering, and association analysis techniques, have already been applied to the educational domain [123]. However, EDM is still an emerging research area, and we can foresee that its further development will result in a better understanding of the challenges specific to this field and will help researchers involved in EDM to see which techniques can be adopted and what new customized techniques have to be developed [121]. Hence, this chapter proposes applying customized EDM techniques to TSM. EDM techniques and methods can be summarized as follows [121]:

- *Prediction*: To infer a target attribute or single aspect of the data from some combination of other aspects.
- *Clustering*: To identify groups of instances that are similar in some respect.
- *Outlier detection*: To discover data points that are significantly different to the rest of the data.
- *Relationship mining*: To identify relationships between variables and encode them in rules for later use.
- *Social network analysis (SNA)*: To interpret and analyze the structure and relations in CSCL tasks.
- *Process mining*: To extract process-related knowledge from event logs recorded by an information system to have a clear visual representation of the whole process.
- *Distillation of data for human judgment*: To represent data in intelligible ways using summaries, visualization, and interactive interfaces to highlight useful information and support decision-making.
- *Discovery with models*: To use a previously validated model (ie, above method, such as prediction or relationship mining) as a component in another analysis.
- *Knowledge monitoring*: To estimate student skills and track student knowledge over time.
- *Non-negative matrix factorization*: To provide a straightforward interpretation in terms of a nonnegative matrix, as the product of two smaller matrices.

Finally, we review a meaningful data mining approach presented in [124], which presents a comprehensive overview of the techniques developed for database-oriented information network analysis. It covers the following key issues:

1. Database as an information network: a data analyst's view.
2. Mining information networks: clustering, classification, ranking, similarity search, and metapath-guided analysis.
3. Construction of informative networks by data mining: data cleaning, role discovery, trustworthiness analysis, and ontology discovery.
4. Evolution analysis, prediction, and diffusion analysis in heterogeneous information networks.
5. Research frontiers in database-oriented information network analysis.

3.2.4 DATA VISUALIZATION

According to Romero et al. [123], interpretation of results is very important for applying the knowledge acquired to making decisions about how to improve the educational environment or system. Therefore the models obtained by the EDM algorithms have to be comprehensible and useful for the decision-making process. In the context of CSCL and security, once trustworthiness decision information is available, e-Learning managers can analyze valid and useful information devoted to reporting security events, improve the framework design, or manage security enhancements.

It is worth mentioning that the EDM methods presented in Section 3.2 include its corresponding data visualization and knowledge discovery approach. In other words, any specific EDM method determines the data visualization model. For this reason, we can consider EDM methods as more general approaches, which also consider data visualization and knowledge discovery.

Regarding specific visualization tools for knowledge discovery, in [121] the authors examined and evaluated the current EDM tools. Here, we summarize the list presented in [121] selecting those tools that are suitable for our context:

- *GISMO* [125]: Graphical interactive monitoring tool that provides useful visualization of students' activities in online courses to instructors.
- *LOCO-analyst* [126]: Educational tool aimed at providing teachers with feedback on the relevant aspects of the learning process taking place in a LMS.
- *PSLC DataShop* [127]: Interactive Web application that allows researchers to rapidly access standard reports, such as learning curves and browsing data.
- *Meerkat-ED* [128]: Toolbox that prepares and visualizes overall snapshots of participants in the discussion forums, their interactions, and the students who are leaders in these discussions.

Finally, since we are considering P2P e-Assessment CSCL activities, we also review representative SNA visualization tools:

- *Cytoscape* [129] is an open source software platform for visualizing complex networks and integrating with any type of attribute data. The platform provides extensions for various kinds of problem domains, including SNA and semantic Web.
- *Gephi* [130] is an interactive visualization and exploration platform for all kinds of networks and complex systems, dynamic, and hierarchical graphs.

3.2.5 DATA ANALYSIS AND VISUALIZATION FOR P2P MODELS

In recent years there has been an increasing amount of literature on complex networks. The authors of [131] reviewed the major concepts and results recently achieved in the study of the structure and dynamics of complex networks and summarized the relevant applications of these ideas in many disciplines. On one hand, scientists have to cope with structural issues, revealing the principles that are at the basis of real networks. On the other hand, many relevant questions arise when studying the dynamics of complex networks, such as learning how the nodes interacting through a complex topology can behave collectively [131]. In our context, we generate a network structure by designing a P2P e-Assessment component and the behavior of the students is analyzed in terms of trustworthiness.

Regarding social network visualization and network graphs, software exists that copes with complex analysis requirements in social networks. According to Ackland et al. [132] many network analysis and visualization software tools exist that are available to collect, analyze, visualize, and generate insights from the collection of connections formed from billions of messages, links, posts, edits, uploaded photos and videos, reviews, and recommendations.

In [133] the authors analyzed social networks and found they are especially concentrated on uncovering hidden relationships and properties of network members. This work used a network analysis based on the forgetting curve to introduce the application of known and proven methods of learning and forgetting into the field of social networks. The forgetting curve was defined in [131] as the probability that a person can recall information at time t since previous recall.

In [133] the authors found that visualization of social networks is a very important part of the whole system network architecture. The visualization tool can quickly provide relevant insight into the network structure, its vertexes, and their properties. In our context of trustworthiness and e-Assessment activities, we can apply network analysis and visualization to assessment goals, such as anomalous student behavior.

3.3 TRUSTWORTHINESS-BASED CSCL

3.3.1 SECURITY IN CSCL BASED ON TRUSTWORTHINESS

Nowadays, ICE solutions based on public key infrastructure (PKI) models [45] are available to offer technological implementations of services, which ensure the security issues that have been described and required in LMSs. PKI, simply defined, is an infrastructure that allows the creation of a trusted method for providing privacy, authentication, integrity, and nonrepudiation in communications between two parties. Otherwise, one of the key strategies in IS is that security drawbacks cannot be solved with technology solutions alone [9]. To date, even the most advanced security technological solutions, such as PKI, have drawbacks that impede the development of complete and overall technological security frameworks. Indeed, current advanced PKI solutions have vulnerabilities that impede the development of a highly secure framework. According to Dark [9], problems encountered in ensuring security in modern computing systems cannot be solved with technology alone.

In addition, the enhancement of technological security models by functional approaches is an alternative research field that yields to interesting approaches. In particular, the application of these approaches to the specific e-Learning field of CSCL is also very relevant and interesting. Among them, trustworthiness analysis, modeling, assessment, and prediction methods are quite promising in the specific context of CSCL [89].

Trustworthiness can be considered as an appropriate functional property in CSCL because most trustworthiness models are based on P2P interactions [10] and CSCL is closely related to student interactions. Although some trustworthiness methods have been proposed and investigated, these approaches have been little investigated in the domain of CSCL with the aim of enhancing security properties. Therefore in this book, we propose to enhance technological security solutions with trustworthiness, through experimenting with methods, techniques, and models, eventually leading to a trustworthiness methodological approach for CSCL [89].

3.3.2 FUNCTIONAL SECURITY APPROACHES FOR CSCL

In order to address more advanced technological security solutions, some authors [9,134] have considered IS as a research topic beyond ICE. The authors in [134] stated that security is both a feeling and a reality. On the one hand, the reality of security is mathematically based on the probability of different risks and the effectiveness of different countermeasures. On the other hand, security is also a feeling, based on psychological reactions to both risks and countermeasures.

Moreover, absolute security does not exist and any gain in security always involves trade-offs between risks, losses, and gains [44], and eventually all security is a trade-off [135]. This view is very relevant because it is based on a hybrid security system in which global technological solutions have to be managed beyond ICE. Moreover, in [9] the authors discussed the fact that problems encountered in ensuring the security of modern computing systems cannot be solved with technology alone. Instead, IS design requires an informed, multidisciplinary approach. Therefore the problem of IS in CSCL is tackled with a functional approach, which combines ICE security solutions with functional models, namely, trustworthiness methods and techniques in CSCL.

Additional CSCL enhancements related to pedagogical factors can be considered based on trustworthiness. According to Hussain et al. [12] the existence of trust reduces the perception of risk, which in turn improves the behavior and willingness to engage in the interactions of the users. In the context of CSCL, interactions between students are one of the most relevant factors in learning performance. Therefore trustworthiness is directly related to CSCL and can enhance the performance of collaborative learning activities. In contrast, IS can encourage and endorse trustworthiness without directly enhancing learning. Another significant difference between IS and trustworthiness, with respect to CSCL, is the dynamic nature of trustworthiness [13]. The behavior of students is dynamic and evolves during the collaborative learning process. While IS is static regarding student behavior, trustworthiness evolves and its assessment can be adapted to behavior changes of students and groups.

3.3.3 FUNCTIONAL SECURITY FOR CSCL BASED ON TRUSTWORTHINESS

Early research works about *trustworthiness management models* [136,137] suggest that soft security, such as social control or user reputation in distributed systems, have to be used to provide security improvements. In this sense, in [136] the authors proposed a social control system devoted to managing security issues when participants themselves are responsible for the security, as opposed to security implemented by external technological solutions. This model is developed by using reputation agents, which manage what information is transmitted to the other actors.

In addition, Abdul-Rahman and Hailes [137] explained why traditional network security mechanisms are incomplete in their capacity to manage trustworthiness and a general model based on recommendations is provided. The authors pointed out that IS solutions need more effective trust management schemes and techniques. They presented the following three trends in current security practice:

1. *Hard security* based on PKI, which is a relevant example of hard security mechanisms though hard security mechanisms do not say anything about trustworthiness.
2. *Centralized protocols*, which use a common trusted authority to form a trust relationship between two mutually distrusting entities. The trusted authority can never be a good enough recommender for everyone in a large distributed system making its credibility depleting. Moreover, its recommendations become uncertain while the community of trustees grows.
3. *Implicit trust assumptions*, which assume that if a secure system is desired, trust assumptions must be explicit and qualification is required, for instance, under what circumstances trustworthiness has been defined.

In order to measure trustworthiness and identify what factors are involved in a quantitative study, in [85] the authors proposed a data provenance trust model that assigns trust scores to both data and data providers based on certain factors that may affect trustworthiness. To this end, Bernthal [11] designed a survey to explore interpersonal trust in work groups identifying trust-building behaviors ranked by order of importance. Following this approach in the e-Learning context, students and their learning resources (eg, shared documents, posts in a discussion forum, etc.) can be modeled when developing CSCL activities. These resources can be used as trustworthiness factors, which can measure trust in those learning activities that students develop. Finally, Abdul-Rahman and Hailes [137] considered different aspects of trustworthiness in terms of expressions and classifications of trust characteristics, such as trust asymmetry, time factor, limited transitivity, and reliability.

3.4 TRUSTWORTHINESS-BASED SECURITY FOR P2P e-ASSESSMENT

3.4.1 ASSESSMENT CLASSIFICATION

The scope of our research, with respect to e-Assessment, is the evaluation model used in UOC Virtual Campus courses. According to UOC [138], the UOC educational model was created with the intention of appropriately responding to the educational needs of people committed to lifelong learning. Regarding the UOC evaluation model, the assessment is a perfect strategy integrated in the learning process, in the sense that it is conceived as a mechanism for learning and giving reciprocal feedback of this process. That is why the UOC assessment is continuous and educational. In this regard, the assessment activities foster the achievement of learning objectives and skill acquisition. In this way, the student can be assessed while doing his/her activity and acquiring skills [138].

The evaluation models used in UOC are classified in accordance with the following four dimensions:

1. type of subject,
2. specific evaluation model,
3. evaluation application, and
4. agents involved in the evaluation processes.

Fig. 3.3 shows factors and evaluation types. Note that a detailed description of these dimensions was presented in the background chapter (see Chapter 2).

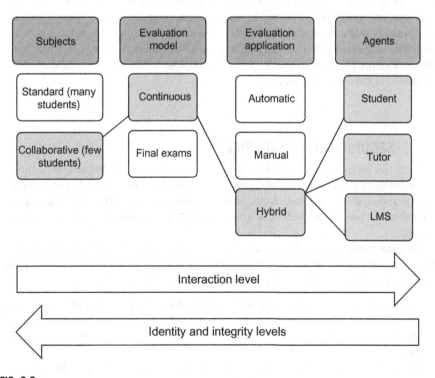

FIG. 3.3

Dimensions and factors for evaluation types.

In our online learning context of UOC, the agents selected are students, tutors, and the LMS, where students carry out learning activities evaluated by tutors in a LMS. Then, two types of subjects are considered: regular subjects based mainly on individual learning and low collaboration among students, and subjects requiring intensive collaboration by small learning teams. Accordingly, two different evaluation models support these subjects: a continuous evaluation model that includes both individual e-Assessment activities during the course and a final exam, and intensive collaborative e-Assessment activities throughout the course and without a final exam.

Once the subject, evaluation model, and agent dimension are introduced, we focus on evaluation procedures. On one hand, in manual evaluation, tutors usually participate directly and intensively in the evaluation process although this creates tedious workload for the teacher when the number of students to evaluate increases up to several hundred. In addition, although manual evaluation may provide higher levels of security because the general interaction between tutors and students is higher than other noncontinuous evaluation models, the interaction level cannot meet security requirements as identification of the student during the interaction may not be authentic. On the other hand, automatic evaluation does not involve direct tutor participation (or just a minimal involvement) and the evaluation process can scale up to larger numbers of students, but cannot support desirable levels of identification and integrity properties. Finally, hybrid evaluation procedures are an interesting combination that can provide a trade-off between manual and automatic evaluation and offer scalability while leveraging high levels of interaction. Fig. 3.3 highlights those elements involved in the proposed model. Our secure e-Assessment model is presented in the following sections.

3.4.2 SECURITY IN e-ASSESSMENT

Henceforth, we move onto security for P2P e-Assessment. Our proposal for enhancing security in e-Assessment through trustworthiness evaluation and prediction has been introduced in previous sections. In this section we summarize significant aspects related to e-Assessment before introducing P2P e-Assessments in the following sections.

In order to determine whether an e-Assessment is secure from the point of view of both students and assessors, inquiry should be made as to whether the e-Assessment satisfies the following general security properties (see Chapter 2):

- *Availability*: e-Assessment activities are available to be performed by the student at the scheduled time and during the time period that has been established. After the activity, the tutor should be able to access the results to proceed to review the task.
- *Integrity*: The description of the e-Assessment (description of the tasks, etc.) must not be changed, destroyed, or lost in an unauthorized or accidental manner. The result delivered by the student must also achieve the integrity property.

- *Identification and authentication*: While performing the evaluation task, the fact that students are who they claim to be must be verifiable in a reliable way. In addition, both student outcomes and evaluation results must actually correspond to the activity that students have performed.
- *Confidentiality and access control*: Students will only be able to access e-Assessment activities that have been specifically prepared for them, and that tutors will access following the established evaluation process.
- *Nonrepudiation*: The LMS must provide protection against false denial of involvement in e-Assessments.

Due to the difficulty of provisioning a completely secure e-Assessment that includes all of these properties, a first approach selects a subset of properties that can be considered critical during the e-Assessment process. The selected properties are identification and integrity, both facing distinct challenges. On one hand, identification must ensure students are who they claim to be during the e-Assessment activities (eg, access to a test description, answering the questions, and submitting the answers, etc.). On the other hand, integrity must ensure both data integrity (ie, the content of the learning activity has not been manipulated before evaluation) and authorship (ie, the content of the learning activity is authored solely by the student or work group). Moreover, authorship presents further challenges as it must fully guarantee the e-Assessment activities have not been influenced or modified by any source external to the student's own knowledge (eg, plagiarism, cheat sheets, unauthorized inputs from peers and experts, etc.).

Finally, e-Assessment activities are mainly performed in an LMS. As information systems, LMSs support two different e-Assessment elements: process and content, both interchangeably related to properties of identification and integrity. Process involves different steps during the dynamic procedure of accessing, performing, submitting, and evaluating the learning activity while content refers to the static activity's outcome going through the procedure steps. Therefore learning services applied to e-Assessment must be considered in both a static and a dynamic way.

3.4.3 SECURE P2P e-ASSESSMENT

Most trustworthiness models in the literature are related to business processes, network services, and recommendation systems [81,86]. The key concept of these works is the interaction between agents, which is the same target that we study in our context of CSCL and networking, considering student P2P interactions and trustworthiness among them (see review of collaborative learning in Chapter 2).

According to Gambetta [81], there is a certain degree of convergence on the definition of trustworthiness, which can be defined as follows: Trustworthiness is a particular level of the subjective probability with which an agent evaluates how another agent (or group of agents) will perform a particular action, before the agent can monitor such action (or independently of the agent's capacity ever to be able to monitor it), and in a context in which it affects the agent's own action. In the context of e-Learning, in [86] the authors stated that a trustworthy e-Learning system is a learning system that contains reliable peers services and trustworthy learning resources.

From the above definitions, trustworthiness can be claimed to be closely related to both student interactions and student actions in networking. Moreover, trustworthiness models are focused on two different dimensions, namely, trustworthiness evaluation and prediction. To establish the difference between trustworthiness evaluation and prediction, in [82] the authors stated that trust prediction, unlike trust evaluation, deals with uncertainty as it aims to determine the trust value over a period in the future. A collaborative activity is a general concept that can involve very different cases, actors, processes, requirements, and learning objectives in the complex context of e-Learning. Therefore both evaluation and prediction are important to P2P e-Assessment.

The context of this section is specifically P2P e-Assessment activities in collaborative learning and networking. We define further e-Assessment as those learning processes that offer opportunities to enhance the student learning experience and its outcomes, such as delivering on-demand tests, providing electronic marking, and immediate feedback on tests [15]. In higher education, e-Assessment is typically employed to deliver formative and summative activities to students, such as an e-Exam. However, LMS in general are reported to suffer relevant issues related to unethical conduct by students occurring during e-Assessment processes [16]. In our networking context, we have endowed e-Assessment activities with trustworthiness evaluation and prediction to enhance security requirements on P2P e-Assessment in LMS [90,139].

To overcome security limitations and drawbacks discussed in this section, we have done investigation on enhancing technological security models with trustworthiness functional approaches [87,88,140].

In [87] we presented a trustworthiness-based approach and proposed the design of secure e-Assessment for small learning groups with high P2P interactions. The guidelines for a holistic security model in online collaborative and P2P learning through an effective trustworthiness approach were presented. Moreover, a parallel processing approach, which can considerably speed up data processing time, was proposed for building relevant trustworthiness models to support e-Assessment, even in real-time (see Chapter 5 for further information). Similarly, in [88] a trustworthiness model for the design of secure P2P learning assessment in online groups was further proposed. To this end, a trustworthiness model was designed in order to lead the guidelines for a holistic security model for CSCL through effective trustworthiness approaches. Finally, in [140] an approach to enhance IS in e-Assessment based on a normalized trustworthiness model was proposed built upon existing normalization procedures for trustworthy values applied to e-Assessment. Eventually, the normalized trustworthiness model was adopted and evaluated in a real CSCL course with many social learning benefits.

3.4.4 **P2P e-ASSESSMENT AND SOCIAL NETWORKS**

Social learning models are also closely related to collective intelligence and P2P networks.

In [79] the authors presented a collaborative tagging system where users assign tags to resources and Web entities. The authors use data from a social bookmarking site intended to examine the dynamics of collaborative tagging systems and to study how coherent categorization schemes emerge from unsupervised tagging. This information is shared with other users and the emerged community's knowledge, due to user interaction. In contrast to this approach of explicit collaboration, in [80] the opposite model is presented and behavior of users is implicitly gathered in order to form a base of knowledge useful for studying tendencies, trends and, therefore, to predict the most useful Web resources.

Both cases presented above illustrate how explicit and implicit models entail a large amount of data from student learning tasks. Hence, we applied parallel computational approaches fully described in Chapter 5 with the aim of overcoming these computational limitations.

In [79] the authors also presented how university students explicitly evaluated the usefulness of several websites, and their browsing activity was gathered. In this comprehensive analysis of collective intelligence, the authors concluded that the correlation indexes suggest the existence of a considerable relationship between explicit feedback and implicit computed judgments. This evidence supports the presentation of a schema for a collaborative application that generates implicit rankings by considering the collective intelligence emerged from users on the Web. Furthermore, regarding our application in P2P e-Assessment, we assume the feasibility of a hybrid approach based on implicit and explicit collaborative data gathering.

3.4.5 **SECURITY LIMITATIONS AND DISCUSSION**

So far we have considered trustworthiness factors from the perspective of students and learning resources and we have also claimed that technological solutions alone cannot solve security requirements. In consequence, all the security methods discussed do not completely ensure e-Assessment activity requirements. Furthermore, neither trustworthiness nor PKI models define what actions to take when the security services detect either anomalous situations or violation of the properties defined. To this end, we must first distinguish between evidence and signs.

On the one hand, security evidence is defined as information generated by the security system in a reliable way which allows for stating that a certain security property has been violated. For example, if an electronic signature process is wrong, we can state that the signed document does not meet the integrity property and this is an irrefutable fact regarding mathematical properties of public and private keys involved in a digital signature. On the other hand, signs allow for assigning a trustworthiness level to a system action or result. These levels are based on

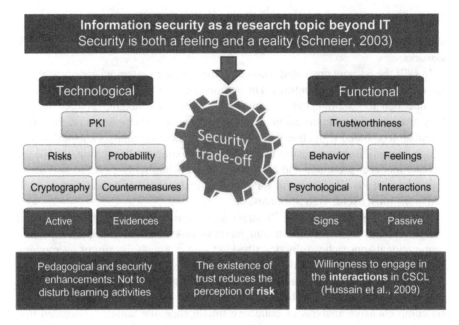

FIG. 3.4

Key concepts related to security in e-Learning and trustworthiness as a functional approach.

probabilities and mathematical calculations, in other words, potential anomalous situations are associated with probabilities.

For each type of anomalous situation detected, it is necessary to define different measures to be taken, as follows:

- *Active*: We act directly on the e-Assessments activities. For instance, if evidence is detected, the security service will deny access to the student and the student cannot continue with the subsequent activities.
- *Passive*: Analysis and audit are focused on analyzing the information provided by the security system without acting on the e-Assessment activities. They may generate further actions, but the process continues as planned before the fault detection.

Fig. 3.4 shows an overview of the topics and related concepts discussed so far, as well as the relationships between IS, security dimensions, e-Learning, functional approaches, technological models, and trustworthiness.

3.5 AN E-EXAM CASE STUDY

In addition to the reasons presented so far regarding tackling the problem of security in e-Learning with functional approaches, in this section we discuss a hypothetical case study which also demonstrates that security for e-Assessment cannot be solved with technology alone.

The e-Exam case study is synchronous and all the students have to access the LMS to take the e-Exam at the same time. The exam procedure is as follows: The description of tasks making up the exam (ie, exam questions) is sent to the students. The questions are the same for all students performing the same e-Exam. Then, each student tries to respond to the questions via a digital document. When the student finishes the exam, the responses are submitted to the LMS before the deadline.

After describing the case used, we show how to improve security requirements using PKI-based solutions, in terms of digital certificates to guarantee the identity of students and for the fulfillment of integrity and authorship security properties. Therefore the process described above is adapted in this way (Fig. 3.5 describes the sequence of tasks):

1. The student accesses the LMS identified by their digital certificate. Similarly, the LMS presents its digital certificate to the student.
2. Since both LMS and student have been identified in a trust process, the student receives the description of the exam and begins to work.
3. The student checks the digital signature embedded in the exam description in order to validate its integrity.
4. When the student finishes the exam, the student performs the operation of digital signature (in the digital document and using their own digital certificate).
5. Eventually, the student's signed document is submitted to the LMS according to the procedure defined in the first step.

Can we trust this model? Are the involved processes and elements of the e-Exam procedure fully satisfying integrity and identity properties? For instance,

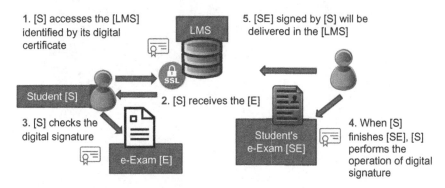

Technological security solutions (PKI) in an e-Exam case study

1. [S] accesses the [LMS] identified by its digital certificate

LMS

5. [SE] signed by [S] will be delivered in the [LMS]

SSL

Student [S]

2. [S] receives the [E]

3. [S] checks the digital signature

e-Exam [E]

Student's e-Exam [SE]

4. When [S] finishes [SE], [S] performs the operation of digital signature

FIG. 3.5

An e-Exam case study based on PKI security techniques.

plagiarism is not detected neither the unauthorized inputs of external sources during the online exam, hence neither satisfy integrity in terms of authorship. Also, by sharing certificate public keys (even signed and issued by a certification authority), any user can replace students and act on behalf of others, thus breaking primary identity properties. Although we can add additional technological measures, such as certificate storage devices, either cryptographic or digital file cards protected by hardware or symmetric cryptography, there are many ways to export these keys or allow remote access to devices that manage the keys, thus making it easy for these vulnerabilities to occur.

We conclude that security in modern computing systems cannot be solved with technology alone. Therefore we find vulnerabilities in this technological security proposal.

Trustworthiness modeling and methodology for secure peer-to-peer e-Assessment

4

4.1 TRUSTWORTHINESS MODELING

4.1.1 NOTATION AND TERMINOLOGY

Before giving some consideration to trustworthiness modeling, we introduce the key terms presented in the following sections (see Table 4.1).

The model presented in this chapter is designed taking into account factors and rules that have been presented in this section. Furthermore, we define two additional concepts (ie, trustworthiness levels and indicators) that are presented in the following sections.

It should be noted that building and reducing trustworthiness factors are closely related to the following (see Table 3.1):

- interactions between participants (eg, TRF-2);
- content management and generation of CSCL results (eg, TRF-1);
- communication processes (eg, TBF-1); and
- group management tasks (eg, TRF-5).

Each of these issues may be involved in e-Learning, but in CSCL learning experiences, we can find a greater number of them than in other learning paradigms. Hence, we focus our trustworthiness model on CSCL.

4.1.2 MODELING TRUSTWORTHINESS LEVELS AND INDICATORS

We now introduce the concept of trustworthiness indicator tw_i (with $i \in I$, where I is the set of trustworthiness indicators) as a measure of trustworthiness factors. Trustworthiness Factors have been presented as those behaviors that reduce or build trustworthiness in a collaborative group; they have been considered in the design of questionnaires. For instance, a trustworthiness indicator measuring the number of messages in a forum is related to the TBF-5 (the student cooperates and looks

Intelligent Data Analysis for e-Learning. http://dx.doi.org/10.1016/B978-0-12-804535-0.00004-6

Table 4.1 Notation and Terminology in Trustworthiness Modeling

TBF_i	Trustworthiness building factor
TRF_i	Trustworthiness reducing factor
TDS	Trustworthiness data sources
tw_i	Trustworthiness indicator
$i \in I$	The set of trustworthiness indicators
Ltw_i	Trustworthiness level
$r \in R$	The set of trustworthiness rules and characteristics
Q	The set of responses in questionnaires
RP	The set of responses in reports
LGI	The set of LMS indicators
RL	The set of ratings in the LMS
$s \in S$	The set of students in the group
n	The total number of trustworthiness indicators
w_i	The weight assigned to tw_i
tw_i^N	Trustworthiness normalized indicator
Ltw^N	Trustworthiness normalized level
$N_j(tw_i)$	Normalization function
$tw_{a_{r,s}}^N$	Normalized indicator
Ltw_i^N	Normalized level
$N_1(tw_{a_{r,s}})$	TBF and TRF normalization function
$N_2(tw_{i,a})$	Group questions normalization function
I_S	The set of indicators for individual assessments
$N_3(tw_i, p_1, p_n)$	Scale conversion normalization function
p_i	Parameters to manage multiple scales
I_R, I_B	The sets of tw_i based on reducing and building factors
$N_4(tw_i)$	Ratings normalization function
T_G	The maximum number of ratings
G	The group of the student s
$N_5(tw_s)$	Group evaluation normalization function
t	The target point in time
tt	The reference point in time
$\overline{tw_i}$	The average of a trustworthiness indicator
$r_{a,t,tt}$	Similarity in points in time for the indicator a
t, tt	Points in time in the learning activity
$r_{a,b}$	Pearson coefficient applied to a target tw_i
tw_a	The target trustworthiness indicator in $r_{a,b}$
tw_b	The reference trustworthiness indicator in $r_{a,b}$
R_{tw}	Individual and group correlation matrix

for mutual help). Therefore an indicator tw_i is associated with one of the measures defined in each e-Assessment instrument (ie, ratings, questionnaires, reports, etc.).

Moreover, we introduce the concept of trustworthiness level Ltw_i as a composition of indicators on trustworthiness rules and characteristics. For instance, we can consider two trustworthiness indicators (tw_a and tw_b). These indicators are different, the first indicator could be a rating in a forum post and the second one could be a question in a questionnaire. However, they measure the same Trustworthiness Building Factor (eg, TBF-1: communicates honestly, described in Table 3.1).

Finally, trustworthiness rules R, may be compared to the group over time or considering the context. Considering all the above, trustworthiness indicators can be formulated by these expressions:

$$tw_{a_{r,s}}, \quad a \in \{Q, RP, LI\}, \quad r \in R, \quad s \in S, \tag{4.1}$$

where Q is the set of responses in Questionnaires, RP is the analogous set in Reports, LI is the set of LMS indicators for each student (ie, ratings and the general student activities in the LMS). S is the set of students in the group and R is the set of rules and characteristics (eg, time factor). These indicators were described above when presenting research instruments.

Once trustworthiness indicators have been selected, trustworthiness levels can be expressed as follows:

$$Ltw_i = \sum_{i=1}^{n} \frac{tw_i}{n}, \quad i \in I, \tag{4.2}$$

where I is the set of trustworthiness indicators that are combined in the trustworthiness level Ltw_i.

Trustworthiness levels Ltw_i must be normalized. To this end, we have reviewed the normalization approach defined in [94] with respect to supporting those cases in which particular components need to be emphasized more than the others. Following this approach, we first need to define the weight vectors:

$$w = (w_1, \ldots, w_i, \ldots, w_n), \quad \sum_{i}^{n} w_i = 1, \tag{4.3}$$

where n is the total number of trustworthiness indicators and w_i is the weight assigned to tw_i.

Then, we define trustworthiness normalized levels as:

$$Ltw_i^N = \sum_{i=1}^{n} \frac{(tw_i \cdot w_i)}{n}, \quad i \in I. \tag{4.4}$$

To sum up, our trustworthiness approach allows for modeling student trustworthiness as a combination of normalized indicators using research and data gathering instruments. Note that in collaborative learning, this same model may also be applied in cases with only one working group. In this scenario, all students would belong to the same group.

4.1.3 STUDENT ACTIVITY DATA SOURCES

Five research instruments are considered to collect user data for trustworthiness purposes and to feed our model:

- *Ratings*: Qualifications of objects in relation to assessments, that is, objects which can be rated or qualified by students in the LMS. Students can share many objects (eg, documents, notes, folders, blogs, etc.), which can be rated in terms of qualification. Therefore we can select the most usual objects that can be rated and that offer a high level of trustworthiness data, namely, posts and collaborative documents. The quality of the CSCL elements can be rated by selecting one of the ratings offered by the LMS.
- *Questionnaires*: Instruments that allow for both collecting student trustworthiness information and discovering general design aspects in our model. In this point, an abstract model of a questionnaire is proposed, which is instanced when the model is implemented. The abstract questionnaire is arranged in five sections (see an excerpt of the questionnaire with the sections in Table 4.2). Each section contains groups of questions of the same type (Questions and Sections, Q/S and questions evaluating the questionnaire, QQ). For each question, the assessment scale is defined. The questions about the group may refer to each member of a group (Group or Individual, G/I and Scale, S). Trustworthiness building and reducing factors are also included as target measurable factors (trustworthiness factor). Finally, the type of the question is defined, the value text (T) means open text responses where students introduce their comments, and if the question is quantitative it is represented by N (number in the scale) or R (if the question is a ranking).
- *P2P evaluation questionnaires*: Continuous evaluation research instruments which collect P2P e-Assessment data.
- *Student reports*: Assessment instrument containing questions and ratings performed by the students and reviewed by the tutors. The student reports are another source of information for trustworthiness. The reports contain questions with quantitative responses. The reports are completed by the coordinator of a group. We suggest two different reports, the first type is public and the group is evaluated, the second one is private (ie, only accessible by the tutor) and contains evaluation data for every member of the group.
- *LMS usage indicators*: To collect the general activity of students in LMS (eg, number of documents created).

All of these research instruments are quantitative and they have been designed to collect mainly trustworthiness levels and indicators as well as assessment information. In order to manage trustworthiness data, we define the concept of trustworthi-

Table 4.2 The Questionnaire Description

QS	GI	TNR	S	Q/S Description	TF
S1	Trustworthiness building factors				
Q1	I	N	1–5	Honest communication	TBF-1
Q2	I	N	1–5	Commitments accomplishment	TBF-3
Q3	I	N	1–5	Confidence in abilities	TBF-2
Q4	I	N	1–5	Regard for partners' statements	TBF-4
Q5	I	N	1–5	Mutual help	TBF-5
Q1–5	I	T	–	Comments regarding Q1,...,Q5	
S2	Trustworthiness, security, and reliability				
Q6	I	R	1–5	Individual trustworthiness level	TBF
Q7	I	R	1–5	Individual security level	TBF
Q8	I	R	1–5	Individual reliability level	TBF
S3	Trustworthiness reducing factors				
Q9	G	T	1–5	Concerned about individual goals	TRF-1
Q10	G	T	1–5	To avoid taking responsibility	TRF-3
Q11	G	T	1–5	To avoid analyzing the facts	TRF-4
Q12	G	T	1–5	To make excuses	TRF-5
Q13	G	T	1–5	To blame others	TRF-5
S4	Risks				
Q14	G	N	1–5	Trustworthiness risk	TRF
Q15	G	N	1–5	Security risk	TRF
Q16	G	N	1–5	Reliability risk	TRF
S5	Evolution				
Q17	G	N	1–5	General evolution	
Q18	I	N	1–5	Evolution in tw level	
Q19	I	N	1–5	Evolution in security level	
Q20	I	N	1–5	Evolution in reliability level	
S6	The questionnaire				
QQ1		N	1–4	Time spent	
QQ2		N	1–5	Size	
QQ3		T		General comments	

ness data sources (TDS). A TDS represents and manages those data generated by the research instrument that we used to define trustworthiness levels, which are presented in the following section.

4.1.4 DATA NORMALIZATION

As presented in the above section, each TDS follows its own trustworthiness data format. Hence, a preliminary normalization process is needed in order to normalize these sources following a unified format. To this end, we introduce the concept of normalized trustworthiness indicator tw_i^N (with $i \in I$, where I is the set of trustworthiness indicators) as a measure of trustworthiness factors. Trustworthiness factors have been presented as those behaviors that reduce or build trustworthiness in a collaborative group. They have been considered in the design of research instruments and data sources.

A tw_i is associated with one of the measures defined in each e-Learning activity or parameter (ie, ratings, questionnaires, reports, etc.) and can be represented following this expression:

$$tw_{a_{r,s}}^N = N\left(tw_{a_{r,s}}\right) a \in \{Q, RP, LI, RL\}, \quad r \in R, \ s \in S, \tag{4.5}$$

where Q is the set of responses in questionnaires (both P2P and individual questionnaires); RP is the analogous set in Reports; LI is the set of LMS general indicators; and RL is the set of Ratings in the LMS. S is the set of students and R is the set of rules and trustworthiness characteristics (eg, time factor).

The Normalization function $N_1\left(tw_{a_{r,s}}\right)$ normalizes the trustworthiness indicator by transforming the indicator value into a unified TDS. Once a value has been normalized, value 1 always means a very low trustworthiness case although the indicator represents, for instance, a TRF or a risk factor. The normalization function considers the normalization of new cases. In other words, as trustworthiness indicators are related to reducing and building factors, function N_1 normalizes all values as trust-building values as follows:

$$N_1\left(tw_i\right) = \begin{cases} \max\left(tw_i\right) - tw_i, & i \in I_R, \\ tw_i, & i \in I_B, \end{cases} \tag{4.6}$$

where I_R is the set of trustworthiness indicators that represent trustworthiness reducing behaviors and I_B is the set of indicators based on building factors.

In a questionnaire, a student can evaluate every member in the group in the same question. We tackle this case with the following normalization function:

$$N_2\left(tw_{i,a}\right) = \sum_{s=1}^{m} \frac{tw_{i,a}}{m-1}, \quad s \neq a, \ i \in I_1, \tag{4.7}$$

where a is the target student (ie, the student which is evaluated); I_S is the set of indicators measuring individual assessments in a student group; and m is the number of students in the group of the student a.

Moreover, we need a linear transformation to convert current scale to the normalized scale 1–5. We propose the linear stretch method [141], as follows:

$$N_3\left(tw_i, p_1, p_n\right) = s_1 + \frac{(s_n - s_1)\left(tw_i - p_1\right)}{(p_n - p_1)}, \tag{4.8}$$

where the primary scale is consecutively numbered from p_1 to p_n and $(s_n - s_1)$ is the target scale, p_1 and p_n are introduced as parameters to manage multiple scales.

Regarding ratings, it is worth mentioning that each group has its own domain and a reference value has to be taken. To this end, we normalize the number of rates that a student has performed, as follows:

$$N_4\,(tw_i) = \frac{tw_i \times (p_n - p_1 + 1)}{T_G}, \tag{4.9}$$

where T_G is the maximum number of ratings by a student in the group G; and $(p_n - p_1 + 1)$ is the number of items in the rating scale.

The last case that requires normalization is related to both student reports and questionnaires. As previously mentioned, public reports evaluate the group and each student is evaluated in public reports, although we have managed a similar case with $N_2\left(tw_{i,a}\right)$ in the case of public reports we do not have individual values. We propose to address this situation by estimating students' values as the group evaluation:

$$N_5\,(tw_s) = tw_G, \quad s \in G, \tag{4.10}$$

where G is the group of the student s and tw_s is an indicator from a public student report.

Finally, we apply each normalization function $N_j\,(tw_i)$ in order to obtain the normalized indicator $N\,(tw_i)$ for those indicators that need normalization by the conditions (ie, in a selective way) presented in this section.

For instance, if we calculate the normalized value of a public student report indicator, the following normalization functions are needed:

$$tw_s^N = N_4\,(N_5\,(tw_s)). \tag{4.11}$$

4.1.5 MODELING NORMALIZED TRUSTWORTHINESS LEVELS

The concept of trustworthiness level Ltw_i is a composition of indicators on trustworthiness rules and characteristics. For instance, we can consider two trustworthiness indicators (tw_a and tw_b). These indicators are different, for example, the first indicator could be a rating in a forum post and the second one a question in a questionnaire. Despite tw_a and tw_b being different indicators, they could measure the same TBF (eg, communicates honestly).

Trustworthiness levels Ltw_i must be normalized. To this end, we select a weight-based normalization approach as normalization model. Following this approach, we previously need to have defined the weight vectors:

$$w = (w_1, \ldots, w_i, \ldots, w_n), \quad \sum_i^n w_i = 1, \tag{4.12}$$

where n is the total number of trustworthiness indicators and w_i is the weight assigned to tw_i.

Overall, we define trustworthiness normalized levels as:

$$Ltw_i^N = \sum_{i=1}^{n} \frac{tw_i \times w_i}{n}, \quad i \in I. \tag{4.13}$$

Therefore, trustworthiness levels allow for modeling student trustworthiness as a combination of normalized indicators using each TDS. Note that a level can be composed of trustworthiness levels, that is:

$$L_i^N = \sum_{i=1}^{n} \frac{Ltw_i^N \times w_i}{n}, \quad i \in I. \tag{4.14}$$

Finally, we consider the time factor as a normalization component, which also allows for analyzing both relation and similarity [98]:

$$r_{a,t,tt} = \frac{\sum_{i=1}^{n} \left(tw_{at,i} - \overline{tw}_{at}\right) \times \left(tw_{att,i} - \overline{tw}_{att}\right)}{\sqrt{\sum_{i=1}^{n} \left(tw_{at,i} - \overline{tw}_{at}\right)^2} \times \sqrt{\sum_{i=1}^{n} \left(tw_{att,i} - \overline{tw}_{att}\right)^2}}, \tag{4.15}$$

where t is the target point in time and tt is the reference point in time (ie, t is compared against tt); tw_a is the target trustworthiness indicator; tw_b is the second trustworthiness indicator in which tw_a is compared (ie, similarity, correlation, anomalous behavior, etc.); $\overline{tw}_a$ and $\overline{tw}_b$ are the average of the trustworthiness indicators; and n is the number of students who provided data for the tw_a and tw_b indicators.

4.1.6 PEARSON CORRELATION ANALYSIS

Following the trustworthiness model presented, we need to inquire whether or not the variables involved in the model are correlated. With this purpose, the correlation coefficient may be useful. Some authors have proposed several methods with respect to rates of similarity, correlation, or dependence between two variables [98]. Even though the scope of [98] is focused on user-based collaborative filtering and user-to-user similarity, the models and measures of the correlations between two items applied in this context are fully applicable in our scope. More precisely, we propose Pearson correlation coefficient (represented by the letter r) as a suitable measure devoted to conducting our trustworthiness model. The Pearson correlation coefficient is a measure of how two variables are linearly related, in other words, a measure of strength of relationship [142]. The Pearson coefficient applied to a target trustworthiness indicator is defined below:

$$r_{a,b} = \frac{\sum_{i=1}^{n} \left(tw_{a,i} - \overline{tw}_a\right) \left(tw_{b,i} - \overline{tw}_b\right)}{\sqrt{\sum_{i=1}^{n} \left(tw_{a,i} - \overline{tw}_n\right)^2} \times \sqrt{\sum_{i=1}^{n} \left(tw_{b,i} - \overline{tw}_b\right)^2}}, \tag{4.16}$$

where tw_a is the target trustworthiness indicator; tw_b is the second trustworthiness indicator in which tw_a is compared (ie, similarity, correlation, anomalous behavior, etc.); $\overline{tw}_a$ and $\overline{tw}_b$ are the average of the trustworthiness indicators; and n is the number of students who provided data for the tw_a and tw_b indicators.

It is important to note that if both a and b are trustworthiness indicators, which have several values over the time (eg, a question which appears in each questionnaire), they must be compared at the same point of time. In other words, it is implicit that $r_{a,b}$ is actually representing r_{a_t,b_t} where a_t is the trustworthiness indicator in time t.

In addition, this test may be applied to every trustworthiness indicator taking one of them as target indicator. To this end, we propose the general Pearson coefficient. The general Pearson coefficient applied to a target trustworthiness indicator over the whole set of indicators is defined as follows:

$$r_{a,t} = \left(r_{a,1}, \ldots, r_{a,i}, \ldots, r_{a,n-1} \right), \quad i \in I, \quad i \neq a, \tag{4.17}$$

where $r_{a,i}$ is the Pearson coefficient applied to a target trustworthiness indicator defined above and I is the set of trustworthiness indicators.

Both relation and similarity are represented by $r_{a,b}$ and r_A grouping students' responses and taking the variables at the same time. We are also interested in the time factor so as to consider the relevant evolution of trustworthiness indicators throughout the course. To this end, we extend previous measures, adding a time factor variable:

$$r_{a,t,tt} = \frac{\sum_{i=1}^{n} \left(tw_{a_t,i} - \overline{tw}_{a_t} \right) \left(tw_{a_{tt},i} - \overline{tw}_{a_t} \right)}{\sqrt{\sum_{i=1}^{n} \left(tw_{a_t,i} - \overline{tw}_{a_t} \right)^2} \times \sqrt{\sum_{i=1}^{n} \left(tw_{a_{tt},i} - \overline{tw}_{a_t} \right)^2}}, \tag{4.18}$$

where t is the target point in time and tt is the reference point in time (ie, t is compared against tt). All other variables have already been defined in this case and they were mentioned twice in the course.

Similarly, we can calculate $r_{a,t,tt}$ for each tt, and then the following indicator may be used:

$$r_{a,t} = \left(r_{a,1}, \ldots, r_{a,i}, \ldots, r_{a,n-1} \right), \quad i \in I, \quad i \neq a, \tag{4.19}$$

The trustworthiness indicators presented in this section are summarized in Table 4.3.

Since hybrid methods are considered to be a suitable trade-off approach for the model, we combine these indicators with the results of a manual continuous evaluation made by the tutor. For instance, a coefficient applied to target trustworthiness indicator a is compared to a manual continuous evaluation, that is:

$$r_{a,b} = cv_t, \tag{4.20}$$

where the second indicator b is exchanged for the value in continuous evaluation.

According to this indicator, we can analyze the similarity between manual and automatic results. Furthermore, each Pearson interpretation that has been presented

Table 4.3 Trustworthiness Basic Indicators

r	Description	Group by	Target
$r_{(a,b)}$	Pearson coefficient applied to a target trustworthiness indicator	Students	tw_a and tw_b
r_a	$r_{(a,b)}$ over the set of indicators	Indicators	tw_a
$r_{(a,t,tt)}$	Pearson coefficient applied to a tw indicator throughout the learning activity from t to tt	Time	tw_a and t
$r_{(a,t)}$	$r_{(a,t,tt)}$ over the learning activity	Activity	tw_a

until now may be applied to continuous evaluations parameters, for instance: $r_{(a,t,tt)}$ where $a = cv_t$.

On the other hand, some questions of the questionnaires that evaluate the same trustworthiness factor are proposed in two different ways: individual and group work evaluation. Hence, students are asked about some factors related to every member of their group and then about the group as a whole. In this case, we can also compare these values using Pearson correlation.

Finally, trustworthiness indicators may be grouped into a trustworthiness matrix with the aim of representing the whole relationship table for each indicator:

$$R_{tw} = \begin{pmatrix} 0 & r_{tw_1,tw_2} & \cdots & \cdots & r_{tw_1,tw_n} \\ 0 & 0 & r_{tw_2,tw_3} & \cdots & r_{tw_2,tw_n} \\ \vdots & \vdots & \ddots & \ddots & \vdots \\ \vdots & \vdots & & \ddots & r_{tw_{n-1},tw_n} \\ 0 & 0 & \cdots & \cdots & 0 \end{pmatrix}. \tag{4.21}$$

Indicators that have been presented in this section are studied in the analysis stage of the model. Although they are proposed as suitable options, the model is refined to select those indicators oriented to perform the best similarity and correlation evaluation model. In addition, this approach is also intended to be a prediction tool, that is, similarity factors may lead to predictions about the evaluation system and its evolution.

4.2 TRUSTWORTHINESS-BASED SECURITY METHODOLOGY

In this section, we first describe the main theoretical features of our methodological approach and then the summary of its key phases is presented. Finally, we detail each phase by analyzing the processes, data, and components involved in the methodology.

4.2.1 THEORETICAL ANALYSIS

Next, we present our methodological approach called trustworthiness and security methodology (TSM) in CSCL. As depicted in Fig. 4.1, TSM is a theoretical approach devoted to offering a guideline for designing and managing security in collaborative e-Learning activities through trustworthiness evaluation and prediction.

TSM is defined in terms of TSM-cycles and phases, as well as components, trustworthiness data, and main processes involved in data management and design. We define a TSM-phase as a set of processes, components, and data. TSM-phases are sequentially arranged in three main phases (see Fig. 4.2) in TSM these form a TSM design and deploy cycle (ie, TSM-cycle). Each TSM-cycle corresponds to an interaction in the overall design process (ie, the three phases form a cycle), in other words, despite the sequential model between each phase, we can consider the overall process, formed by these three phases, as a TSM-cycle. A TSM-cycle allows e-Learning designers to improve the collaborative learning activities from the results, and trustworthiness decision information retrieved from the previous TSM-cycle.

Firstly, these concepts are presented as a methodological approach and then we complete the theoretical analysis with those methods and evaluation processes.

TSM aims to deliver solutions for e-Learning designers. To this end, TSM supports all analysis, design, and management activities in the context of trustworthiness collaborative learning activities, reaching security levels defined as a part of the

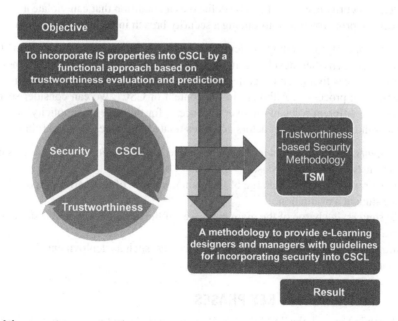

FIG. 4.1

Trustworthiness-based Security Methodology main objective and result.

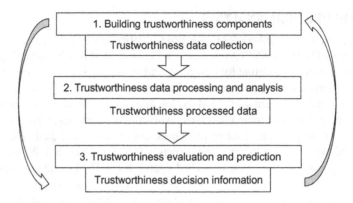

FIG. 4.2

Trustworthiness and Security Methodology main phases.

methodology. Therefore TSM tackles the problem of security in CSCL through the following guidelines and main goals:

1. define security properties or services required by e-Learning designers;
2. build secure CSCL activities and design them in terms of trustworthiness;
3. manage trustworthiness in learning systems with the aim of modeling, predicting, and processing trustworthiness levels; and
4. detect security events that can be defined as a condition that can violate a security property, thus introducing a security breach in the learning system.

The scope of our methodological approach is an e-Learning system formed by collaborative activities developed in an LMS. The LMS has to provide support to carry out these activities and to collect trustworthiness data generated by learning and collaboration processes. Although in the context of CSCL we can consider several actors with different roles in the overall process, for the sake of simplicity, we only consider the most significant actors and roles related to this research, as follows:

1. *Students*: the main actors in the collaborative learning process and as targets of the trustworthiness analysis.
2. *Teachers and tutors*: in charge of the main processes of the learning, specially, the student's evaluation.
3. *Designers*: in charge of the main processes of the learning, especially student evaluation.
4. *Managers*: that develop management processes, such as deployment, monitoring, or control tasks.

4.2.2 METHODOLOGY KEY PHASES

As shown in Fig. 4.2, the TSM methodology is divided into three sequential phases:

1. *Building trustworthiness components*, integrated into the design of secure collaborative learning activities.

2. *Trustworthiness analysis and data processing*, based on trustworthiness modeling.
3. *Trustworthiness evaluation and prediction*, to detect security events and to refine the design process.

Although we assess each phase of the methodology as potential sets of concurrent processes (see the following sections), these core phases have to be developed following the sequential phases presented. The main reason for defining this sequential model is the input and output flow. In other words, the output of one phase is the input of the next one. For instance, we can only start the data collection phase when trustworthiness components are deployed. Likewise, we cannot start trustworthiness prediction or assessment until data processing has been completed.

We consider the overall process, formed by these three phase, as a TSM-cycle. Each TSM-cycle allows e-Learning designers to improve the collaborative learning activities from the results, and trustworthiness decision information retrieved from the previous cycle. This information can introduce design enhancements which will be deployed in the next deployment (ie, the next time that the students carry out the activity supported by the learning component). In terms of the data flow between TSM-cycles, the input for the new design iteration is the trustworthiness decision information. For instance, if decision information shows that a deficiency exists in a component, the detected impediment can be overcome through design changes that are deployed in the next TSM-cycle execution.

4.2.3 BUILDING TRUSTWORTHINESS COMPONENTS

The first phase of TSM deals with the design of collaborative activities. The key challenge of the design process is to integrate trustworthiness data collection into the learning process. In other words, the trustworthiness component has to carry out its learning purpose. In addition, the learning component has to produce basic trustworthiness data. Moreover, data collection methods and processes should not disturb the learning activity. To this end, we propose the processes, data, and components that can be seen in the diagram in Fig. 4.3. Since the first goal of the methodology is to design the trustworthiness component, we divide this phase into the following analysis considerations:

1. Collaborative learning activities generate a significant amount of interactions. Since student interactions are closely related to trustworthiness modeling, designers have to consider and analyze each interaction related to trustworthiness.
2. Analyzing and determining relationships between student interaction and trustworthiness could be a challenging task in e-Learning design. Hence, we propose the study of trustworthiness factors (see Section 3.1.2), which can be defined as those behaviors that reduce or build trustworthiness in a collaborative group. Trustworthiness factors can be divided into TRFs and TBFs. This resource will allow designers to determine those interactions that may generate basic trustworthiness data.

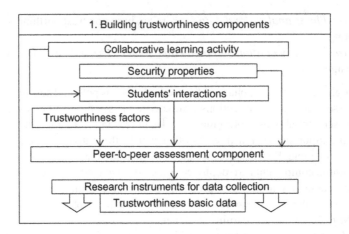

FIG. 4.3

Phase 1: Building trustworthiness components.

3. Designers have to model security issues so that they are compatible with trustworthiness data and student interactions.

Based on the above considerations, we propose the analysis of general security properties and services presented. Through selecting and analyzing security properties we can connect trustworthiness, interactions, and security requirements in terms of collaborative learning activities.

From the study of security properties, student interactions, and trustworthiness factors, the initial collaborative learning activity has evolved to a P2P assessment component. Once we endowed the collaborative activity with security and trustworthiness, the next process is focused on data collection. To this end, we define research instruments for data collection intended to retrieve all trustworthiness data generated by the P2P assessment component.

Note that, for the sake of simplicity, we present a case dealing with one collaborative activity only, which generate its P2P assessment component. However, this case may be extended to a set of collaborative activities implemented in one or several P2P components. Moreover, the components can be supported by several research instruments or a P2P component, including multiple collaborative activities. Eventually, the result (ie, single and multiple activities, components, and instruments) is a set of basic trustworthiness data that will feed the next phase of the methodology. For this reason, we define the input of the next phase in terms of multiple TDS.

We also propose the need for modeling activities, components, security properties, or interactions in the context of a general design process. This process may be a challenge if the e-Learning designer does not use suitable modeling tools. To overcome this impediment, we reviewed the educational modeling languages

[48] that, with the indications presented in Section 2.2.4, allows designers to tackle modeling security, CSCL activities and interactions.

4.2.4 TRUSTWORTHINESS ANALYSIS AND DATA PROCESSING

So far, our e-Learning designer has built the trustworthiness component, which will be deployed in the LMS. It is worth mentioning that the deployment of collaborative learning activities may involve multiple LMSs. In fact, we propose a learning activity deployment in conjunction with research instruments for data collection. The implementation of these instruments may require additional technological solutions such as normalization processes. Trustworthiness modeling and normalization processes in TSM (see Fig. 4.4) are based on the key concepts presented in this chapter.

We introduced the concept of the trustworthiness indicator as a measure of trustworthiness factors. Trustworthiness factors were presented (see Section 2.2.4) as those behaviors that reduce or build trustworthiness in a collaborative activity and they were integrated in the design of research instruments. Therefore we define a trustworthiness indicator as a basic measure of a trustworthiness factor that is implemented by a research instrument and integrated in the P2P assessment component. Finally, trustworthiness levels can be defined as a composition of trustworthiness indicators. The concept of levels is needed because trustworthiness rules and characteristics must be considered and, consequently, we have to compose this more complex measure.

Regarding normalization functions, there are several reasons that impede the management and processing of trustworthiness levels directly. Among them, we can

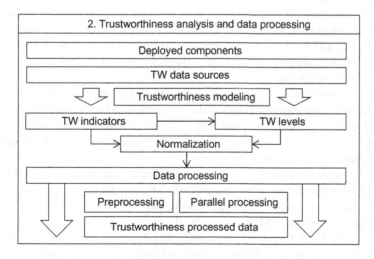

FIG. 4.4

Phase 2: Trustworthiness analysis and data processing.

highlight several aspects, such as multiple sources, different data formats, measuring techniques and other trustworthiness factors, such as rules, trustworthiness evolution, or context. Therefore both trustworthiness indicators and levels have to be normalized through normalization functions. The selection of these functions depends on the data sources and the format selected for each instrument of data collection.

Once trustworthiness modeling concepts are defined, the task of data processing starts, and then basic data from TDS is computed in order to determine indicators or levels, for each student, group of students, evaluation components, etc. The main challenge of data processing in this case is that extracting and structuring these data are a prerequisite for trustworthiness data processing. In addition, with respect to computational complexity, extracting and structuring trustworthiness data is a costly process. Moreover, the amount of basic data tends to be very large. Therefore techniques to speed and scale up the structuring and processing of basic trustworthiness data are required for a parallel implementation approach to be developed in the context of trustworthiness data processing. The parallel processing model will be presented in Chapter 5.

4.2.5 TRUSTWORTHINESS EVALUATION AND PREDICTION

From the trustworthiness data computed in the previous phase, we can carry out both evaluation and prediction processes, which allow e-Learning managers to make security decisions based on the output of this phase (ie, trustworthiness decision information). Furthermore, this information can be taken into account as input data for an iterative design process as mentioned in Section 4.2.2.

Trustworthiness evaluation and prediction stem from the analysis of the time factor in trustworthiness. Fig. 4.5 shows how trustworthiness evaluation and prediction begin with the conversion of processed data into trustworthiness sequences by considering the time factor. The concept of a trustworthiness sequence is related to levels and indicators and can be defined as the ordered list of a student's normalized levels of trustworthiness when the student is performing the P2P assessment component over several points in time.

Once trustworthiness sequences are built, the e-Learning manager is able to set out predictions and assessment processes. As presented in Section 3.1.6, methods intended to predict and assess trustworthiness are available in the context of P2P assessment. The e-Learning designer has to select and determine suitable methods for the specific target scenario.

We cannot use trustworthiness decision information (ie, reliable trustworthiness information) without the validation process. The validation process is intended to filter anomalous cases, to compare results that represent the same information from different sources, and to verify results using methods, such as similarity coefficients. Nevertheless, this information may indicate signs. and the complex nature of trustworthiness modeling requires additional validation processes. These validation models can be classified into internal and external, and each type may involve automatic and manual tasks. For instance, in the context of e-Assessment, we

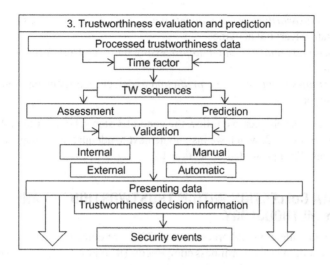

FIG. 4.5

Phase 3: Trustworthiness evaluation and prediction.

could compare trustworthiness results generated by the P2P assessment component to external results (regarding to the P2P component) from the manual tutor evaluation. Moreover, this comparison could be automatically developed by the system and analyzed by the tutor before taking any decision.

Finally, trustworthiness decision information is available and then e-Learning managers can analyze valid and useful information devoted to reporting security events, improve the framework design, or manage security enhancements. In Chapter 6 we will present specific TSM aspects in real online courses, focused on trustworthiness evaluation and trustworthiness prediction.

4.3 KNOWLEDGE MANAGEMENT FOR TRUSTWORTHINESS AND SECURITY METHODOLOGY

In this section we show the enhancing TSM with knowledge management aspects (refer to knowledge management (KM), learning analytics (LA), educational data mining (EDM) and other related topics in Chapter 3).

As described in the previous section, TSM is defined in terms of TSM-cycles and phases. We define a TSM-phase as a set of processes, components, and data. TSM-phases are sequentially arranged and the three main phases form a TSM design and deploy cycle (ie, TSM-cycle). Each TSM-cycle corresponds to an interaction over the design process. TSM supports all analysis, design, and management activities in the context of trustworthiness collaborative learning activities, reaching security levels defined as a part of the methodology. TSM is divided into three sequential phases:

1. *Building Trustworthiness Components* integrated into the design of secure collaborative learning activities.
2. *Trustworthiness analysis and data processing* based on trustworthiness modeling.
3. *Trustworthiness evaluation and prediction* to detect security events and refine the design process.

In the rest of the chapter, we follow the general 3-step schema of the KM process presented in Section 3.2, which we instantiate next to adequately manage trustworthy data within our TSM presented in Section 4.2.

4.3.1 DATA COLLECTION WITHIN TRUSTWORTHINESS AND SECURITY METHODOLOGY

Regarding data collection and processing in TSM, we consider two phases in TSM. In particular, building trustworthiness components (ie, phase 1, see Section 4.2.3) and trustworthiness data processing and analysis (ie, phase 2, see Section 4.2.4) including processes and components related to data collection and processing.

These components and processes are highlighted in Figs. 4.6 and 4.7.

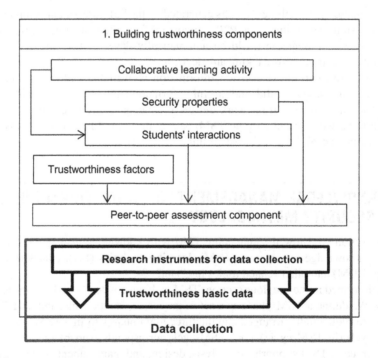

FIG. 4.6

Building trustworthiness components, data collection design.

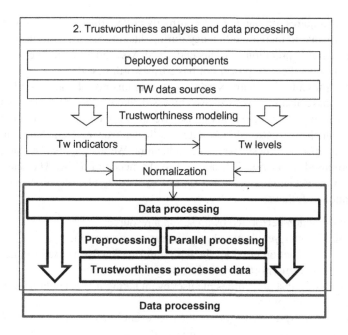

FIG. 4.7

Trustworthiness analysis, data collection deployment.

As shown in Fig. 4.6, we consider design issues as a foremost step in trust-worthiness data collection. The key challenge of the design process is to integrate trustworthiness data collection into the learning process. The design process involves the following considerations:

1. The determining of relationships between student interaction and trustworthiness.
2. The study of trustworthiness factors in interactions in order to generate basic trustworthiness data.
3. The modeling of security issues so that they are compatible with trustworthiness data and student interactions.

These design decisions will determine the success of the computational model. Research instruments for data collection generate basic trustworthiness data. These instruments have to facilitate computational requirements in deployment phases.

4.3.2 DATA PROCESSING WITHIN TRUSTWORTHINESS AND SECURITY METHODOLOGY

Following the process presented in Section 3.2, the e-Learning component has to be designed in a way that classifies and prestructures the resulting information.

This process requires, on one hand, to correctly collect the group activity data and, on the other hand, to increase efficiency during data processing in terms of analysis techniques and interpretations. To this end, the e-Assessment component design has to support the classification process of basic trustworthiness data.

Fig. 4.7 presents the main process and components of the second phase of TSM. This phase also involves trustworthiness data collection processes, which are highlighted in the diagram. In this phase, we incorporate in TSM a classification process, in which the trustworthiness data is collected from existing data sources, and processed as trustworthiness levels and indicators. We also apply the classification process proposed in Section 3.2, adapted to the needs of TSM. The data sources are handled in sequential steps consisting of extraction, identification, coding, and categorization as follows:

1. Extract the action performed by a user on a resource.
2. The action is interpreted according to its type of user event.
3. The interpreted action provides the basic information that is used for the composition of trustworthiness indicators and levels.
4. The processing system codifies the user event taking into account both the user action and the event type.
5. The processing system categorizes the user event into one of the group activities following the security and trustworthiness design.

4.3.3 DATA ANALYSIS WITHIN TRUSTWORTHINESS AND SECURITY METHODOLOGY

As introduced in Section 3.2, EDM provides methods and techniques, which are suitable solutions for enhancing our KM process approach. Once the processes involved in trustworthiness analysis and data processing have been performed, the next phase of TSM (ie, trustworthiness evaluation and prediction) considers data analysis methods related to EDM. Although, as shown in Fig. 4.8, trustworthiness evaluation and prediction were considered as essential components of TSM, this initial approach is now enhanced with EDM general models. In Fig. 4.8 we have divided the processes and components of this phase of TSM into two categories, namely, data analysis (ie, the *Analysis* step in KM) and visualization (ie, the *Presentation* step in KM). Once the categories have been identified, we endow our KM with the following EDM techniques:

- *Prediction*: Trustworthiness prediction supports the detection of security events and refining of the design process, by anticipating e-Learning security problems before these events have occurred.
- *Clustering*: Trustworthiness evaluation based on level and indicators requires the analysis of trustworthiness factors. These factors are those behaviors that reduce or build trustworthiness in a collaborative group. From this point of view,

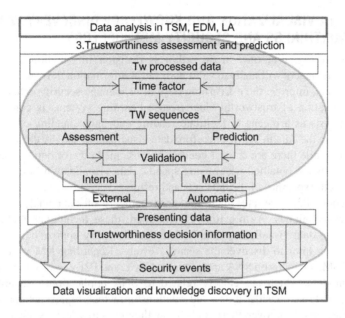

FIG. 4.8

Data analysis and visualization, EDM in TSM.

clustering is a suitable technique to identify groups of factors that are similar as regard trustworthiness building and reducing factors.

- *Outlier detection*: Anomalous user e-Assessment detection is one of the key requirements of CSCL security based on trustworthiness. Since with this technique it is feasible to discover data points that are significantly different to the rest of data, outlier detection supports the detection of anomalous user e-Assessment.

- *Relationship mining*: CSCL is based on the interactions and relationships between students. Relationship mining techniques identify relationships between variables and normally encode them in rules for later use. Therefore if student interactions are accurately modeled, relationship mining allows for enhancing the trustworthiness evaluation process.

- *Social network analysis*: Due to TSM being focused on P2P e-Assessment, SNA is a suitable improvement for TSM in order to interpret and analyze the structure and relations in CSCL activities.

- *Process mining*: CSCL activities are developed in LMSs, which produce events stored in log files. Hence, the extraction process of knowledge from event logs recorded by an information system is a feasible capability in TSM.

To sum up, these EDM techniques are suitable solutions for enhancing trustworthiness evaluation and prediction in TSM.

4.3.4 DATA VISUALIZATION AND KNOWLEDGE DISCOVERY WITHIN TRUSTWORTHINESS AND SECURITY METHODOLOGY

As shown in Fig. 4.8, once trustworthiness decision information is available, e-Learning managers will analyze valid and useful information devoted to reporting security events, improve the e-Learning design, or manage security enhancements. Data visualization of trustworthy data from e-Learning systems is commonplace in data analysis as a means to facilitate reading and understanding of the results extracted from the data in TSM. Therefore data visualization usually closes the cycle of the KM. While there are several generic-purpose methods for data visualization, the best results are obtained when using specific data visualization in order to take into account the specifics of the data sets and results.

In Section 4.3.3 we presented the enhancements of data analysis in TSM with EDM techniques. As previously mentioned, these techniques include their corresponding data visualization and knowledge discovery approach, which allow the e-Learning tutor to discover the security events. Regarding KM visualizations tools for TSM, we focus on SNA applications. CSCL and P2P e-Assessment produce network models, which are closely related to SNA applications. Regarding the network model, we consider a directed relationship, which represents that $student_1$ assessed $student_2$. Moreover, these tools allow the tutors to select a student and then the tutors analyze and discover the map of connections for each student.

Regarding visualization tools, NodeXL [143] is an open source software tool especially designed to facilitate learning the concepts and methods of SNA with visualization as a key component [144]. Moreover, in [133,145] the authors proposed an online analysis tool called Forcoa.NET, which is focused on the analysis and visualization of the co-authorship relationship based on the intensity and topic of joint publications. The visualization of co-authorship networks allows for describing the author and her current surroundings, while still incorporating historical aspect. The analysis in Forcoa.NET is based on using the aforementioned forgetting function [131] to hold the information relevant to the selected date. After this analysis, several measures can be computed with the aim of describing different aspects of user behavior from the point of view of scientific social networks.

Before studying a specific tool for data visualization in TSM, it is useful to present specific cases of online courses and data management models, which are detailed in the next chapter.

4.4 BUILDING STUDENT PROFILES IN e-ASSESSMENT

4.4.1 COLLECTIVE INTELLIGENCE

According to Mazzara et al. [78], although several definitions of collective intelligence have been proposed, a shared agreement suggests that Collective Intelligence is a group or shared intelligence that emerges from the collaboration and or competition of many entities, either human or digital. Previous research works [78–80] demonstrated how the resulting information generated by models based on collective intelligence can be seen as reflecting the collective knowledge of a community of users and can be used for different purposes.

Collective intelligence, via information sharing among trusted agents, can be analyzed from two different perspectives. On one hand, social networking is globally expanding and lacks a specifying and implementing of appropriate security and privacy procedures to protect user data [78], thus requiring technological IS solutions in order to reach social networking privacy and security requirements. On the other hand, collective intelligence and social networking involves trustworthiness relationships between the agents in the system. Hence, trustworthiness evaluation and prediction can enhance security in collaborative frameworks.

In [146] the authors stated that collective intelligence communities often struggle to grow large enough to achieve their goals. This problem is frequently characterized as a problem of critical mass. Dealing with critical mass with the aim of helping those trying to start communities (ie, in the early stage of the community) involves the following issues [146]:

- Individual communities often have different patterns of growth.
- Building membership has a greater impact on community activity in later periods than accumulating many contributions early on.
- Participation from a community's *power users* is not as valuable to sustainability as the collective contributions of those who make only small contributions.
- Critical mass is established by developing a diverse set of members with heterogeneous interests and resources, and not purely by accumulating content.

For these reasons, student groups should be carefully analyzed and monitored due to the complexity of reaching the critical mass of the student learning community.

4.4.2 STUDENT TRUSTWORTHINESS PROFILE

In an e-Learning system based on collective intelligence, trustworthiness propagation is needed in order to support both e-Assessment and collaborative learning activities, such as creating student groups. As stated by the authors in [147], trust is considered as the crucial factor for agents in decision making to select partners during their interaction in open distributed systems. To this end, the author presented a computational model that enables agents to calculate the degree of trustworthiness of partners as well as enabling agents to judge the trustworthiness of the referee when basing trust in a partner on a referral from its referees, thus preventing agents from giving referrals to the reputation of liar agents.

In our context of online collaborative learning, a first relevant activity requires the creation of learning groups. Trustworthiness can support this crucial process. Most current trust models are the combination of experience trust and reference trust, and make use of some propagation mechanism to enable agents to share students' trust with their partners. These models are based on the assumption that all agents are reliable when they share their trust with others [147]. Therefore among these mechanisms, student profiles can be a suitable approach with the aim of supporting trustworthiness propagation in the e-Learning system.

Since we propose the design of a collective intelligence application (CIA) (ie, student profile application), we first review the main principles in designing CIA. In [148] the authors presented the seven principles [149] that were adapted to the CIA requirements. This approach can be summarized as follows:

- *Task-specific representations*: CIA should support views of the task. CIA is data centric (ie, data is key) and should be designed to collect and share data among users.
- *User-added value*: CIA should provide mechanisms for users to add, to modify, etc. with the aim of improving its usefulness.
- *Facilitate data aggregation*: CIA should be designed such that data aggregation occurs naturally through regular use.
- *Facilitate data access*: Data in CIAs can be used beyond the boundaries of the application. CIA should offer Web services interfaces and other mechanisms to facilitate the re-use of data.
- *Facilitate access for all devices*: CIA needs to be designed to integrate services across hand-held devices and Internet servers.
- *The perpetual beta*: CIA is an ongoing service provided to its users, thus new features should be added on a regular basis based on the changing needs of the user community.

Some LMSs include a service intended to support the management of student profiles, however, these services are not designed with the aim of managing either trustworthiness or collective intelligence data gathering. For instance, Moodle [52] as a representative LMS system, which is being extensively adopted by educational organizations to help educators create effective e-Learning communities, supports the management of student profiles as follows [150]:

- Students can see their peer and tutor profiles in the course.
- Course managers and administrators can access and edit student profiles.
- Users can view and manage their own full profile.

User profiling in Moodle offers a basic set of functions that does not reach CIA requirements presented in this section. Even those related to collaborative learning activities cannot be developed using Moodle student profiles. Despite these limitations, Moodle offers additional modules devoted to the enhancement of collaborative activities, for instance, Moodle badges are a suitable way of showing achievement and progress as they are based on a variety of criteria. Moodle badges are fully compatible with other systems and can be displayed on a user profile [150].

Therefore most representative LMSs, such as Moodle, can offer collective intelligence tools and services based on student profile, which can be taken as a starting point. However, they do not reach CIA requirements and cannot offer an overall technological solution to support a student's security profile model for e-Assessment based on trustworthiness and collective intelligence.

In addition, contributions from literature on profiling students include an adaptive computer assisted assessment system that automatically scores students and gives feedback to them based on their responses and the questions chosen according to their student profile and previous answers [151]. Another interesting approach determines student academic failure through building student profiles with data mining methods [152]. This profile approach is based on information extracted from online surveys filled out by the students and the data analysis is conducted by classification methods. Although both studies address a specific goal related to e-Assessment applications (ie, student responses in surveys and previous answers in e-Assessments), and the proposal is based on student profiles, they are conducted by assessment components, which do not support collaboration and collective intelligence.

To the best of our knowledge, current student profiling approaches are specifically focused on concrete objectives, which cannot be extended to the scope of collective intelligence, trustworthiness, and security in e-Assessment. Therefore further on this chapter, we make a proposal on how to apply previous research presented in this section to student profiles with the aim of enhancing security in e-Assessment through trustworthiness and collective intelligence.

4.4.3 COLLECTIVE INTELLIGENCE FOR e-ASSESSMENT IN CSCL

Considering the previous approaches on student profiles based on collective intelligence, from this point on we present our model of student profiling based on e-Assessment, collective intelligence, CSCL, and trustworthiness evaluation and prediction, aiming at endowing our previous TSM presented in Chapter 3 with a student trustworthiness profile (STP) approach based on collaborative learning, e-Assessment activities, and collective intelligence processes. We address the profiling design for trustworthiness evaluation and prediction as well as for enhancing security in e-Assessment.

Although in Chapters 6 and 7 we will detail the e-Assessment activities and their development in real online courses, in this section we depict one of these activities with the aim of discussing the design of the student profiles based on collective intelligence. Collective intelligence principles have been presented above in the background section. In this section we adapt these principles to e-Assessment in CSCL. To this end, we consider the continuous assessment (CA) P2P e-Assessment component which can be depicted as follows:

1. *Questionnaire Q*: The student receives an invitation to answer a set of questions.
2. *Forum F*: A forum F is intended to create a collaborative framework devoted to enhancing responses in Q.
3. *P2P survey P*: This is used by students to assess the responses of each classmate in Q as well as the activity of each student in the forum F.

As can be seen from the CA description above, the assessment result emerges from the collaboration of many students who carry out collaborative learning activities and e-Assessment processes. Collective intelligence principles are considered in CA design as follows:

- *Task-specific representations*: The e-Assessment activity supports multiple views of the task. The responses of the questions proposed are involved in each activity of the assessment process. The first question is individual while the second one has a collaboration target. Finally, every response is presented as a result, which has to be assessed.
- *Data is the key*: We consider that student responses are the data collected and shared among students. Moreover, since students assess each other's responses in Q, we state that the students add value to both the system and the original data.
- *Facilitate data aggregation*: The activities Q and P are quite static, whereas the forum activity F is dynamic and open. Therefore the forum activity allows students to carry out data aggregation.
- *Facilitate data access*: Mechanisms to facilitate the re-use of data are implemented in our CA model by developing an interface that automatically generates the activity P from data collected in activity Q (ie, responses in Q are the assessment target).
- *Facilitate access for all devices*: The CA does not require advanced technological systems or devices. The only requirement is a Web browser and an Internet connected device.
- *The perpetual beta*: The CA component is designed with the aim of being repeated several times in the course. For each iteration, the CA is enhanced following decision information generated by the e-Assessment processes.

The CA offers e-Assessment processes based on collective intelligence and online collaborative learning. However, this model is an isolated e-Learning component since each iteration does not remember or refer to previous history. In other words, when students perform a certain P2P survey P, they do not consider previous activity or past results of the student who is currently assessing. Because this drawback impedes the overall trustworthiness analysis in our model, we propose a profile based approach. Moreover, students assess individual values (ie, responses of other students) but cannot the trustworthiness information of their classmates.

4.4.4 PROFILES BASED ON COLLECTIVE INTELLIGENCE

We address our profile-based approach to collaborative e-Learning knowledge and e-Assessment analysis purposes by considering that the collective intelligence emerged from the group of students is the student profile. The student profile collects, stores, and publishes the student's trustworthiness information, such as the CA data based on collaborative e-Assessment results. During the above sections, the main design decisions, rules, and features of the collective intelligence approach for trustworthiness-based student profile were presented as depicted in Fig. 4.9.

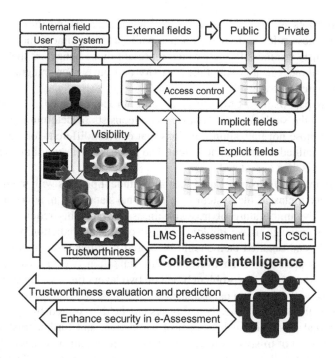

FIG. 4.9

Collective intelligence for STP.

Following the process defined for the CA development (ie, incorporation of the student profiles to the model), the CA design has to be modified in order to add such components and processes required to reach the following profile goals:

1. collect trustworthiness student information;
2. trustworthiness modeling and assessment;
3. store student information in their profile in a persistent form; and
4. publish computed trustworthiness values.

We next detail these processes following our TSM approach (see Chapter 3 for full details of how trustworthiness data is collected modeled and normalized by the TSM methodology).

Within the TSM, the main concepts related to trustworthiness data collection are research instruments and data sources. Following the example of CA, we consider that a P2P survey is a research instrument, which collects responses in Q and generates the scores for each student while data sources define the format, source, and input processes for each search instrument.

Then, once basic trustworthiness data have been collected, this source has to be processed in order to generate more complex and useful trustworthiness values in terms of indicators and levels. Trustworthiness levels are a composition of indicators on trustworthiness rules and characteristics while trustworthiness indicators are a measure of trustworthiness factors, which represent those behaviors that reduce or build trustworthiness in a collaborative activity and have been integrated into the design of research instruments.

Finally, as part of the TSM, a normalization process is needed before adding these data into the student profile. This process consists of determining, selecting, and applying those normalization functions that convert different formats and data sources into a unified measurement system. The process of trustworthiness modeling and evaluation is then completed.

At this point, and following Fig. 4.9, storing student profiles with the implementation of either a classic file system or a relational data base may seem a simple task, but the dynamic nature of trustworthiness converts this requirement into a challenge. For instance, if we implement trustworthiness prediction processes, the previous basic and detailed data should be stored in order to compare and verify trustworthiness predictions. To overcome this limitation, we propose a trade-off solution to tackle the storage problem based on two layers (ie, user layer and system layer) for trustworthiness data persistence.

Moreover, the internal layer contains system fields required by the system to develop internal processes such as control, validation, and further trustworthiness evaluation. The set of trustworthiness indicators and levels must be carefully defined due to the potential limits in storage size and computational cost. In addition to control, processing, and internal design requirements, the design based on user and system layers of trustworthiness levels has two major purposes related to students and tutors functional aspects.

The first layer (ie, user layer) involves user fields and is based on collective intelligence in online collaborative learning. The user layer provides a presentation layer devoted to publishing student trustworthiness levels. These levels are a significant source of information when students are developing collaborative activities (eg, the process of a learning group creation) and e-Assessment processes (eg, evaluating the quality of a classmate's response in a questionnaire).

The internal user layer covers fields for hybrid evaluation methods. We have proposed hybrid methods as a trade-off combination, which can provide a balance between the degree of interaction and security requirements regarding manual and automatic evaluation methods. This model requires additional information that cannot be published in the external student layer. For instance, whereas the trustworthiness history levels may be a private value in the student context, tutors need to know and assess these values with the aim of comparing manual and automatic results.

Finally, the trustworthiness levels and indicators are published in the student profiles. In this case, we consider two publication rules that are presented in the following sections. Namely, privacy and security rules related to the design of the profile and the LMS integration issues.

4.4.5 **TECHNOLOGICAL SECURITY SETTING FOR STUDENT PROFILE**

As mentioned in the background section, technological and functional security approaches are closely related. Specific trustworthiness profile applications can involve particularly technological issues due to the nature of students' assessment information. A key step is to define the visibility and access rules for student profile fields, mandatory data, optional data and private data that can only be accessible by special LMS users, such as tutors (Fig. 4.9).

In addition, due to ethical aspects, e-Assessment and trustworthiness data have to be managed according to the law, responsiveness, and the protection of privacy principles established for each educational institution. Students should also decide whether they prefer not to publish certain information. To this end, we propose a customization control access module intended to offer a student profile visibility configuration tool. This tool should be developed as an integrated module in the LMS.

Finally, ICE security solutions are needed in order to meet social networking privacy and security requirements. For this reason, we propose to include ICE security fields into the student profiles. An ICE security field can be defined as the information representing the ICE security level that the student usually uses in the LMS. For instance, a low ICE security level could be an identification process based on classical login and password procedure while a high ICE security level might be a student signing a message with a digital certificate (ie, an advanced PKI solution).

4.4.6 **EXPLICIT AND IMPLICIT TRUSTWORTHINESS INFORMATION**

The development of the learning activities involves certain aspects that can be analyzed in terms of either explicit or implicit trustworthiness information. On one hand, explicit trustworthiness information refers to the development of learning activities involving behavioral aspects that can be analyzed in terms of trustworthiness. For instance, when students assess a classmate's response or when a group of students are discussing a topic in a forum, they are generating explicit trustworthiness information. On the other hand, implicit trustworthiness information is related to collaborative and e-Assessment activities, which generates trustworthiness and collective intelligence information, that are not directly related to trustworthiness factors and behaviors, but can still be taken into account for defining profile fields. For instance, if a student spends a relevant amount of time reading discussions in collaborative documents, the LMS can monitor this action and this fact can be indirectly interpreted as a TBF.

However, implicit information brings further issues derived from automatic and real time approaches when processing and presenting this information. Indeed, the computational cost has to be considered and reduced in order to provide effective and just-in-time implicit trustworthiness information from the LMS. Continuous processing and analysis of student activity are required during their learning activity, which produces huge amounts of valuable data typically stored in server log files.

In Chapter 5 we study the computational cost limitation with a parallel processing proposal, which can considerably decrease the time for data processing, thus allowing for building relevant trustworthiness models to support learning activities even in real-time.

Finally, even if we assume that the model is suitable, the parallel processing reduces the computational cost and implicit trustworthiness information is automatically included and published in the student profile, this process does not ensure that implicit information is reliable. For instance, a student who knows that the system is monitoring certain LMS use parameters may deceive the system with the help of a Web injection software application to simulate a real learning activity in the LMS. To overcome this problem, we propose to compare data from multiple sources. In Chapter 3 we presented validation data based on Pearson correlation coefficient as a suitable measure devoted to conducting our trustworthiness model by comparing implicit and explicit trustworthiness fields. If validation tests do not meet the set thresholds, the implicit trustworthiness information will not be included in the student profile.

4.4.7 SUMMATIVE EVALUATION ON STUDENT PROFILE AND SERVICES

So far, our student trustworthiness profiling model can be summarized as TSP services, fields, and goals.

The TSP is formed by a set of quantitative fields with the following features:

- TSP field design is based on two layers.
- A TSP field can be implicit or an explicit field.
- TSP fields are based on trustworthiness, e-Assessment and collective intelligence.
- A TSP field may contain ICE security information.

In addition, we include three services intended to manage, maintain, and monitor the TSP: data validation processes, access control, and student visibility tools. To this end, we focus on collaborative activities, e-Assessment activities, and collective intelligence processes. Finally, TSP applications aim at addressing the profile design in order to provide trustworthiness evaluation and prediction and to enhance IS in e-Assessment.

In addition to the overall TSP guidelines proposed in this section, we can consider trustworthiness levels related to the group and the course. This approach may allow the course managers and tutors to assess and predict results regarding the overall learning process and specifically with respect to the group's activity.

4.5 CASE STUDY: AUTHENTICATION FOR MOOC PLATFORMS

As an application of our TSP methodology to a popular learning scenario, in this section we discuss the use of TSP specifically for satisfying the authentication properties of MOOC platforms. To this end, we first elicit the requirements for our model from a hypothetical case study on MOOCs described next.

4.5.1 CASE DEFINITION

As presented in Chapter 2, MOOCs are defined as open, free, participatory, and distributed courses, representing a new generation of online education, easily and widely accessible on the Internet and involving a large or very large number of students [65]. Current deliverers of MOOCs are very concerned about this user authentication issue and make great efforts to know and verify the student identity during the MOOC sessions. For instance, they use biometrics (eg, typing patterns) and other complicated mechanisms, which sometimes prove to be unreliable and are often privacy intrusive [71]. This also becomes a particular issue for satisfying accrediting institutions and hiring companies that rely on the emergent MOOC educational phenomenon [70,72].

Innovative user authentication methods for verifying MOOC student identity are required, so that the course progress and results are not compromised by either incompetence or malice [73]. Providing security to MOOC, and in particular effective student authentication (ie, ensuring that students are who they say they are), has been claimed by some authors as an essential feature in the MOOC arena, especially for evaluation, grading and eventual certification purposes [71,74].

4.5.2 PROVIDING SECURITY TO MOOCS e-ASSESSMENT

An e-Learning platform delivers a MOOC named *Applying security on IT projects* focused on information technology (IT) targeting students who are interested in IS improvements applied to IT projects. A short summary of this MOOC is provided below:

- It is offered as a part of the Open University of Catalonia (UOC) Open Programs initiative and deployed into UOC OpenCourseWare [153].
- Unlimited number of participants.
- Includes self-assessment and peer-assessment activities, and a final automatic test.
- After successful accomplishment of the course the student receives credits and an official certificate issued by UOC.

In this scenario it is essential to verify student identity during the course, particularly when e-Assessment activities are performed, thus also satisfying UOC's accrediting requirements. To meet these requirements, we propose a modular PKI-based security model called MOOC smart identity agent (MOOC-SIA) as the main component that manages different authentication methods in the MOOC platform in a centralized fashion.

Fig. 4.10 depicts an architectural view of our solution and an example application for our case study. In order to explain this architectural view, we show a use case example.

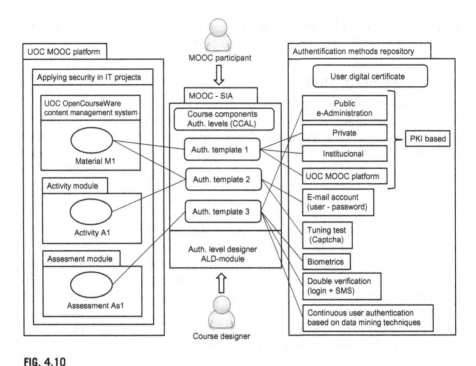

FIG. 4.10

The MOOC-Smart Identity Agent model.

Firstly, the course designer, who is working on a specific assessment activity, creates a new CCAL by using the ALD module and selecting the most suitable authentication methods for this particular assessment (see the above figure). To this end, the course designer selects public PKI (eg, Spanish DNI-e [154]), double verification (eg, firstly, login and password and then an additional code sent to the participant before the login process) and a biometric method (eg, participant's fingerprint).

Due to the high degree of student interaction during MOOC sessions, we take great advantage of the tracking-based techniques of user modeling, such as providing broader and better support for the users of online educational systems. Our purpose is to constantly track the short-term interaction of a student with the MOOC platform and then compare it to the student's historical or long-term profile/user model by using data mining techniques in order to look for potential deviations (anomalous authentication). The required data for tracking can be collected to a large extent from information kept in log data files of the MOOC platform (involving IP, time stamp, user navigation and other log data). This information is then analyzed and adequately interpreted in order to extract the knowledge needed to build the desired user model for our purpose of user authentication [155].

4.5.3 DISCUSSION

Our MOOC-SIA model provides a flexible authentication system to meet each and every type of course and user profile. Course designers can choose the most suitable authentication methods and compose effective authentication instances for each activity, content or assessment. Moreover, these authentication instances are reusable by means of templates (see Fig. 4.10). On the other hand, there are certain LMSs, which even if supporting multiple authentication methods, cannot be applied simultaneously by user, method, etc. Moreover, MOOC-SIA implementation and integration into existing LMS may be a challenge.

In addition, the provision of real-time user tracking for student verification in MOOCs by using data mining techniques involves processing large amounts of information of a great variety of types and formats [156]. Moreover, MOOC sessions are characterized by a high degree of user-user and user-system interaction, which produces huge amounts of valuable data typically stored in server log files. As a consequence, treating this information is very costly in time and space, thus requiring high performance computational power.

Finally, although the requirements for our TSP methodology have been elicited from a hypothetical case study and these requirements are involved in an actual UOC scenario, there are further variables which should also be considered in order to test the accuracy of the MOOC-SIA model. Among these variables, we may consider the amount of data to be processed and training time of the system.

Massive data processing for effective trustworthiness modeling

5

5.1 OVERVIEW ON PARALLEL PROCESSING

5.1.1 PARALLEL PROGRAMMING MODELS

The most important research works about parallel programming models were first summarized in [157]. This early classification follows a decreasing order of abstraction:

1. Models that abstract from parallelism completely, describing only the purpose of a program. This is the simplest model for software developers, since they do not have to know whether the program will execute in parallel or sequential.
2. Models in which parallelism is made explicit, but decomposition of programs into threads is implicit. Software developers do not consider implications for decomposition, mapping, communication, and synchronization between threads.
3. Models in which parallelism and decomposition must both be made explicit, but mapping, communication, and synchronization are implicit. Such models require decisions about the breaking up of processing work into pieces, but they relieve the software developer of the implications of their programming decisions.
4. Models in which parallelism, decomposition, and mapping are explicit, but communication and synchronization are implicit. In this model software developers have to consider how to place the pieces of work on the designated node. Since this model requires an awareness of the computing architecture, software portability across different architectures becomes complicated.
5. Models in which parallelism, decomposition, mapping, and communication are explicit, but synchronization is implicit. Almost all the implementation decisions correspond to software developers, except for timing decisions dealing with synchronization.

Intelligent Data Analysis for e-Learning. http://dx.doi.org/10.1016/B978-0-12-804535-0.00005-8

6. Models in which everything is explicit and software developers must specify every implementation detail.

As a matter of fact, these categories are still valid and thus we consider the factors described in the classification process in the rest of the chapter. However, the specific parallel processing approaches of these models have to be upgraded. Therefore in the rest of this section we explore the actual landscape of parallel processing approaches and frameworks.

5.1.2 PARALLEL PROCESSING FOR DATA-INTENSIVE VS COMPUTING-INTENSIVE APPLICATIONS

Parallel processing approaches can be generally classified as compute-intensive, data-intensive or both [157–159]. Data-intensive applications face two major challenges [158]: processing exponentially growing data volumes and significantly reducing data analysis cycles with the aim of making timely decisions. While compute-intensive is used to describe application programs that are compute-bound, such applications devote most of their execution time to computational requirements as opposed to input/output, and typically require small volumes of data [159]. Finally, data-intensive and compute-intensive are usually those applications that have both features.

The classification between data- and compute-intensive parallel processing is also related to the concept of grid computing. A computing grid is typically heterogeneous in nature (ie, different computing nodes), and consists of multiple geographically distributed nodes using wide area networking communications. Grids are typically used to solve complex computational problems which are compute-intensive. In contrast, data-intensive computing systems are tackled with homogeneous clusters (ie, nodes in the computing cluster are identical) and use local area communications between nodes [159]. Grid computing served as a basis for the emergence of cloud computing due to its ability to virtualize resources, which is the basis for cloud computing services. Although cloud computing is not necessarily bound to parallel processing, cloud models based on infrastructure or platform as a service are directly applicable to data-intensive parallel computing [160].

A cloud service typically includes a large pool of configurable virtual resources that can be scaled to accommodate varying parallel processing loads [161]. The concept of big data is also related to parallel computing approaches. Big data is the next frontier for innovation, competition, and productivity, and many solutions continue to appear, supported by the considerable enthusiasm around the MapReduce paradigm [162].

Regarding parallel computing memory architectures, there are shared, distributed, and hybrid shared-distributed memories [163]. Shared memory architectures are based on global memory space, which allows all nodes to share memory. In distributed memory architectures, processors have their own memory and they have a communication network and protocol to connect each computation node. Finally, hybrid shared-distributed memory combines both shared and distributed memory architectures.

5.2 PARALLEL MASSIVE DATA PROCESSING

The theory of parallel computing is concerned with the development and analysis of parallel computing models, the techniques for solving and classifying problems in such models, and their use for solving real life problems [164]. Parallel computing involves different disciplines. For this reason, in 2006, a diverse group of researchers from the University of California at Berkeley, from various backgrounds related to parallel computing, developed a technical report called *The Landscape of Parallel Computing Research: A View From Berkeley* [165]. This multidisciplinary research group was formed by expert researchers on programming languages, instruction set architectures, interconnection protocols, circuit design, computer architecture, massively parallel computing, embedded hardware and software, compilers, scientific programming, and numerical analysis. One major conclusion of this report was that, since real world applications are naturally parallel and hardware is naturally parallel, what we need is a programming model, software system, and a supporting architecture that are naturally parallel.

In addition, the main reasons and advantages for parallel computing and the reasons why parallelism is a topic of interest are [157]:

1. The real world is inherently parallel, thus it is natural to express computing about the real world in a parallel way, or at least in a way that does not preclude parallelism.
2. Parallelism makes more computational performance available than is available in any single processor, although getting this performance from parallel computers is not straightforward.
3. There are limits to sequential computing performance that arise from fundamental physical limits.
4. Parallel computing is more cost-effective for many applications than using sequential models.

To exemplify the study, this chapter uses the MapReduce model and Hadoop framework, as parallel programming architectures and disciplines (see also Chapter 2 for further information). To this end, we will consider hardware and computer architecture topics, which are closely related to the particular MapReduce cluster implementation and deployment, while our purpose is to efficiently process massive data and use the analysis results to eventually enhance security in e-Learning.

5.2.1 PARALLEL PROCESSING FOR P2P STUDENT ACTIVITY

In Chapter 3, we presented a trustworthiness-based approach for the design of secure learning tasks in e-Learning groups. To this end, we justified the need to improve internet security (IS) in e-Learning and, in particular, in CSCL tasks. Then, we proposed a methodological approach to building a security model for CSCL tasks with the aim of enhancing standard technological security solutions with trustworthiness factors and rules. As a result, we proposed the guidelines of a holistic security model in online collaborative learning and P2P learning tasks through an effective trustworthiness approach. However, since learner trustworthiness analysis involves a large amount of data generated during learning tasks, processing this information is computationally costly, especially if required in real-time. With the aim of alleviating this limitation, we developed and tested a parallel processing approach that can considerably decrease the data processing time, thus allowing for the building of relevant trustworthiness models to support learning tasks even in real-time.

In the rest of this chapter, from the case presented in Chapter 3, we first review the main parallel models and the MapReduce approach. Then, we discuss the main factors and implementation details involved in a Hadoop MapReduce implementation for the analysis of P2P data from student learning tasks. The processing of student activity results will allow the tutors to manage e-Learning security events, as well as online visualization through P2P tools.

5.2.2 THE COMPLEXITY OF PROCESSING LARGE LOG FILES

The process of extracting and structuring LMS log data is a prerequisite for later key knowledge management processes (see Chapter 3), such as the analysis of interactions, assessment of group activity, or the provision of awareness and feedback involved in CSCL [114–116].

The computational complexity of extracting and structuring LMS log files is a costly process as the amount of data tends to be very large and needs computational power beyond that of a single processor (see Fig. 5.1 and [114,115]). In addition, in [116] a study was also done on the feasibility of processing very large log data files from the virtual campus of the Open University of Catalonia (UOC Virtual Campus) using different distributed infrastructures to examine the time performance

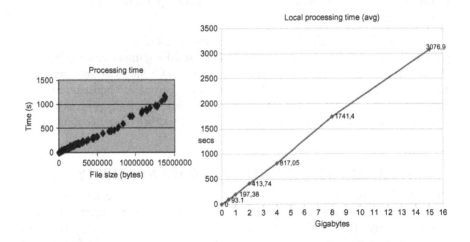

FIG. 5.1

Sequential processing of two LMS log files of the real virtual campus.

of massive processing of log files. It was also shown that processing time for local processing of UOC log files is linear with respect to log data size (see Fig. 5.1), hence, the computational cost of sequentially processing large amounts of log data becomes unfeasible.

Therefore parallel techniques to speed and scale up the structuring and processing of log data are required when dealing with log data. In [116,156] these models were implemented following the master-slave paradigm and evaluated using cluster computing and Planet Lab platforms [166].

Taking these approaches as a starting point, in this chapter we extend our goals in two different directions: (i) parallelizing the normalization of several LMS log files and (ii) using MapReduce paradigm for efficient processing of normalized data.

5.3 THE MapReduce MODEL AND Hadoop

5.3.1 THE MAPREDUCE PROGRAMMING PARADIGM

In recent years, the MapReduce framework has emerged as one of the most widely used parallel computing paradigms [167,168]. The MapReduce framework was originally proposed by Google in 2004, since then, companies such as Amazon, IBM, Facebook, and Yahoo! have adopted the MapReduce model [169].

According to Dean et al. [167], MapReduce is a programming model and an associated implementation for processing and generating large data sets. The model is based on specifying a *Map* function that processes a key/value pair to generate a set of intermediate key/value pairs, and a *Reduce* function that merges all intermediate values associated with the same intermediate key. The Map/Reduce functions are as follows [167]:

- The *Map* function takes an input pair and produces a set of intermediate key/value pairs. The MapReduce library groups together all intermediate values and passes them to the *Reduce* function.
- The *Reduce* function accepts an intermediate key (produced by the *Map* function) and a set of values for that key. It merges together these values to form a smaller set of values. Typically, just zero or one output value is produced per *Reduce* invocation.

Fig. 5.2 shows a schema that illustrates the MapReduce main features and basic flow process.

5.3.2 MAPREDUCE IN PARALLEL COMPUTING CLASSIFICATIONS

Regarding the parallel computing model and classification discussed in Section 5.1, MapReduce programs are automatically executed in a parallel cluster-based computing environment [167]. The run-time framework takes care of the details of partitioning the input data, scheduling the program's execution across a set of

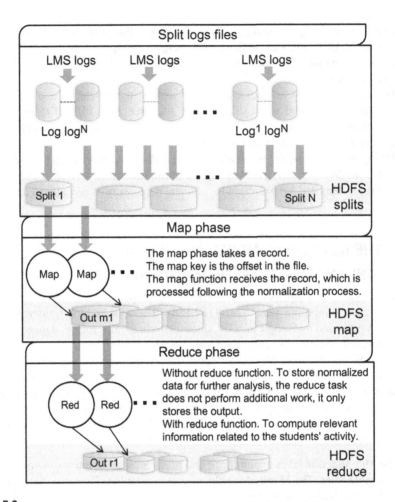

FIG. 5.2

MapReduce basic schema.

machines, handling machine failures, and managing the required intermachine communication. This allows programmers, without any experience with parallel and distributed systems, to utilize the resources of a large distributed system [167]. In other words, the MapReduce model arises as a reaction to the complexity of the parallel computing programming models, which consider the specific parallel factors involved in software development processes.

5.3.3 Hadoop ARCHITECTURE

The Apache Hadoop software library is a framework devoted to processing large data sets across distributed clusters of computers using simple programming models.

It is designed to scale up from single servers to thousands of machines, each offering local computation and storage [170]. Although the Apache Hadoop project includes many Hadoop-related projects, the main modules are the Hadoop MapReduce and Hadoop distributed file system (HDFS).

HDFS supports large data-sets across multiple hosts to achieve parallel processing. HDFS is a block-structured file system based on splitting input data into small blocks of fixed size, which are delivered to each node in the cluster.

The Apache Hadoop NextGen MapReduce, also known as Apache Hadoop yet another resource negotiator (YARN), or MapReduce 2.0 (MRv2), is a cluster management technology. The fundamental idea of MRv2 is to split up the two major functionalities of the JobTracker into resource management and job scheduling. The idea is to have a global resource manager and per-application master. The resource manager and per-node slave manager (ie, node manager) form the data-computation framework. The resource manager is the authority that arbitrates resources between all the applications in the system. The per-application master is in charge of negotiating resources from the resource manager and working with the node managers to execute the tasks [171].

The HDFS is the primary distributed storage used by Hadoop applications. A HDFS cluster consists of a name node that manages the file system metadata and data nodes that store the actual data [172].

5.3.4 **MapReduce AND Hadoop CASE STUDIES**

In [119] the authors present a collection of Hadoop case studies contributed by members of the Apache Hadoop community. Among them, we summarize the most significant case studies.

Last.fm [173]

There are about 25 million users of Last.fm, generating huge amounts of data. These data need to be processed, stored, and allow the users to access them directly. Moreover, the data are used to make decisions about user preferences. Hadoop has become a crucial part of Last.fm infrastructure, currently consisting of two Hadoop clusters spanning over 50 machines, 300 cores, and 100 TB of disk space. Hundreds of daily jobs are run performing operations such as log file analysis and chart generation.

Facebook [174]

The amount of log data in Facebook that needs to be processed and stored has exploded and a key requirement for Facebook is the ability to scale rapidly. Furthermore, the engineering resources are limited and the system needs to be very reliable, as well as easy to use and maintain. With the aim of tackling this limitation, the Facebook team explored back-end data architectures and the role Hadoop can play in them. As a result, the cluster size is more than 2 PB of data in Hadoop and it loads more than 10 TB of data every day. Regarding the cluster usage, the Hadoop instance has 2400 cores, about 9 TB of memory, and runs at 100% utilization at many points during the day.

Rackspace Hosting [175]

This company provides managed systems and email services for enterprises. Rackspace currently hosts email for over 1 million users and thousands of companies on hundreds of servers. This Hadoop cluster contains 15 nodes with three 500-GB disks each. From a MapReduce programming perspective, each line of the log is a single key-value pair. The *Map* function groups all lines with a single queue-id key, and then the *Reduce* phase determines if the log message values indicate that the queue-id is complete.

5.3.5 Hadoop CLUSTER INFRASTRUCTURE

As presented in Section 5.3.3, we can consider Hadoop in general terms as a framework, a software library, a MapReduce programming approach or a cluster management technology. Behind these general models, a cluster infrastructure has to be included as a crucial part of the general framework. In the case of Apache Hadoop there are custom services and cluster infrastructure solutions devoted to offering a comprehensive parallel processing framework for MapReduce applications. Therefore in this section, we look at the main features offered by the Apache Hadoop project for cluster infrastructure requirements.

The Hadoop documentation project offers a specific manual about Hadoop Cluster Setup [176]. This manual describes how to install and configure Hadoop clusters and the management services that are available in the global framework. The most important issues discussed in this manual are:

- The cluster requires exclusive machines for master services, *NameNode* and *ResourceManager*.
- The existence of additional control services deployed in dedicated machines, *Web App Proxy Server* and *MapReduce Job History Server*.
- The rest of the machines in the cluster are slave nodes, *DataNode* and *NodeManager*.
- Hadoop provides services for monitoring the cluster health and failover controls. The cluster administrators can customize these options by defining functions that notify the state of each node.
- If a node's status is reported as unhealthy the node is blocked and no further tasks will be assigned to this node. However, the monitoring process continues and, when the node becomes healthy again, it will be available for processing tasks. Hence, this model not only provides failover controls, but also increases the performance level of the cluster.
- The components are rack-aware regarding network topology and storage model. The administrator defines the rack information, and then the cluster provides data and network availability based on the cluster characteristics.

- Once the cluster is configured and running, the cluster administrators can use Web applications for operating the management services, *NameNode*, *ResourceManager* and *MapReduce JobHistory Server*.

In addition to the cluster infrastructure defined above, there is an additional project intended to enhance the cluster management services, namely, Apache ZooKeeper [176] enables highly reliable distributed coordination. According to The Apache Software Foundation [176], ZooKeeper is a centralized service for maintaining configuration information, naming, providing distributed synchronization, and providing group services. The main goals and guarantees of ZooKeeper are summarized in [176] as follows:

- *Sequential consistency*: Updates will be applied in the order that they were sent.
- *Atomicity*: Updates either succeed or fail, that is, the system avoids partial results.
- *Single system image*: A client will see the same view regardless of the server to which it is connected.
- *Reliability*: Once an update has been applied, it will persist.
- *Timeliness*: The clients view of the system is up-to-date within a defined time bound.

5.3.6 OTHER PARALLEL PROGRAMMING FRAMEWORKS

In this section we review other parallel computing and programming frameworks.

OpenMP application program interface (OpenMP API) is a shared memory multiprocessing application program inference for easy development of shared memory parallel programs. It provides a set of compiler directives to create threads, synchronize the operations, and manage the shared memory [177]. OpenMP threads management is based on the POSIX threads standard (Pthreads), which is defined as a set of interfaces (functions and header files) for threaded programming. These threads share the same global memory (data and heap segments), but each thread has its own stack (automatic variables) [178]. The programs using OpenMP are compiled into multithreading programs [163].

According to the official MPI-3.0 standard [179], message passing interface (MPI) is a message passing library interface specification. MPI addresses primarily the message-passing parallel programming model, in which data is moved from the address space of one process to that of another process through cooperative operations on each process. Specific implementations of MPI exist, such as OpenMPI, MPICH and GridMPI [180].

As seen in the main conclusions presented in surveys of parallel programming models [180] and performance comparison studies [163], OpenMP is the best solution for shared memory systems, MPI is the convenient option for distributed memory systems, and MapReduce is recognized as the standard framework for big data processing.

5.4 MASSIVE PROCESSING OF LEARNING MANAGEMENT SYSTEM LOG FILES

5.4.1 OPEN UNIVERSITY OF CATALONIA VIRTUAL CAMPUS LOG FILES

Before presenting our parallel processing implementation approach, we first show the different format of LMS log files and the problems of processing them due to their large size and the ill-structured formats of both. To this end, a normalization approach for both types of log data is proposed as an input to our general parallel processing model presented in following sections.

In the context of the UOC, general e-Learning activities are supported by Web-based services in the UOC Virtual Campus, while the collaborative activities are supported by a popular collaborative platform called basic support for cooperative work (BSCW). BSCW is a fully-fledged Web-based collaboration platform that facilitates efficient teamwork through a wide range of functions [181]. In this section we first review the case of the UOC virtual campus log files. Then, in Section 5.4.2 we analyze the BSCW logs.

The BSCW service completes the UOC Virtual Campus offering a collaborative learning environment and supporting the complexity of the collaborative learning practices that involve hundreds of undergraduate students and a dozen tutors. Moreover, with the aim of capturing the group interaction, we use the above-mentioned BSCW as a shared work-space system, which enables both collaboration requirements and data collection features. Therefore we propose the use of BSCW with a twofold purpose, namely, to support complex collaborative learning activities, and to collect trustworthiness information (ie, events, collaborative items, ratings, etc.) for security analysis.

The Web-based Virtual Campus of the UOC is made up of individual and community virtual areas such as mailbox, agenda, classrooms, library, secretary's office and so on. Students and other users (lecturers, tutors, administrative staff, etc.) continuously browse these areas where they request services to satisfy their particular needs and interests. For instance, students make strong use of email service so as to communicate with other students and lecturers as part of their learning process.

The user requests in the UOC Virtual Campus are chiefly processed by a collection of Apache [182] Web servers as well as database servers and other secondary applications, all of which provide service to the whole community and thus satisfy a great deal of user requests. For load balance purposes, all hypertext transfer protocol (HTTP) traffic is smartly distributed among the different Apache Web servers available. Each Web server stores all user requests received in this specific server and the information generated from processing the requests in a log file. Once a day (namely, at 1:00 am), all Web servers, in a daily rotation, merge their logs producing a single very large log file containing the entire user interaction with the campus performed in the last 24 h. A typical daily log file size may be up to 20 GB. This great amount of information is first preprocessed using filtering techniques in order to remove a lot of futile, nonrelevant information (eg, information coming from automatic control processes, the uploading of graphical and format elements, etc.). However, after this preprocessing, about 2.0 GB of potentially useful information a day corresponding to 5,000,000 log entries on average still remains [156].

The log files storing the entire activity of the UOC Virtual Campus follow the Apache log system. A typical configuration for the Apache log system is the common log format [183]. A standard configuration for this log system is:

```
LogFormat "%h %l %u %t \"%r\" % > s %b" common
```

where *h* is the Internet protocol (IP) address of the client or remote host, *l* indicates unavailable requested information, *u* is the user identification name, *t* is the time that the server finished processing the request, *r* is the request line, *s* is the status code and *b* is the size of the object returned.

In the UOC Virtual Campus, log file records are managed following a variation of the common log format known as combined log format [183], with two additional fields:

```
LogFormat "%h %l %u %t \"%r\" %>s %b \"%{Referer}i\"
          \"%{User-agent}i\"" combined
```

where *Referer* field shows the site that the client reports have been referred from, and *User − agent* field identifies information that the client browser reports about itself.

As an example, the following is a record that is part of a real log from the UOC Virtual Campus (IP address has been anonymized):

```
[15/Mar/2012:00:26:40 +0100] xxx.xxx.xxx.xxx
"POST /WebMail/listMails.do?mensajeConfirmacion=
     ******************************************
       HTTP/1.1"
200 "http://cv.uoc.edu/WebMail/readMail.do"
"Mozilla/4.0 (compatible; MSIE 7.0; Windows NT 6.1;
             Trident/5.0; SLCC2; .NET CLR 2.0.50727;
             .NET CLR 3.5.30729; .NET CLR 3.0.30729;
             OfficeLiveConnector.1.3; OfficeLivePatch.0.0;
             InfoPath.2; BRI/2)"
8857 20A
```

This example record illustrates that the user id parameter described in Apache combined log format is not available in this line. Moreover, neither unavailable requested information *l* nor the size of the object *b* meet the standard arrangement. Although user identifications are not stored in log files, the system maintains a session id, this value is a user session key (a 128-character long string) included as a parameter in the request.

At this point, we highlight certain issues arising when dealing with processing of these log files:

1. We cannot uniquely identify either the user or the record.
2. Each explicit user request generates at least one entry in the log file but it usually generates additional requests, for instance, in order to compose a user Web interface, each component (ie, image, style sheets, etc.) will be loaded using GET operations. This information is not relevant and these records unnecessarily increase both the storage space and processing effort.

3. Additional parameters introduced in combined format (referer and user-agent) may be useful for audit purposes, but in our context these values introduce a high degree of redundancy.

However, certain limitations can be overcome. Although the user cannot be identified uniquely, log record identification is possible by combining several fields as a record key. The parameters selected to identify a record are represented in the following tuple:

$$\text{Record}_{\text{Key}} = (\text{IP}, \text{Time}, \text{Session}), \tag{5.1}$$

where IP is the address of the client or remote host, Time is the time that the server finished processing the request and Session is the session key or id generated by the client's request.

Moreover, redundant and unnecessary information can be parsed and ignored.

The above actions have been implemented as described in the following sections following a record taxonomy devoted to cleaning unusable data. Moreover, regarding storage space, we next propose the most efficient way to store record data.

5.4.2 BASIC SUPPORT FOR COOPERATIVE WORK LOG FILES

In our real learning context of the UOC, several online courses are provided involving hundreds of undergraduate students and a dozen tutors in a collaborative learning environment. The complexity of the learning practices entails intensive collaboration activity generating a great amount of group activity information. To implement the collaborative learning activities and capture the group interaction we use the above-mentioned BSCW as a shared work-space system, which enables collaboration over the Web by supporting document upload, group management and event service among other features. BSCW event service provides awareness information to allow users to coordinate their work [184].

In the BSCW, the events are triggered whenever a user performs an action in a work space, such as uploading a new document, downloading (ie, reading) an existing document, renaming a document, and so on. The system records the interaction data into large daily log files and presents the recent events to each user. In addition, users can request immediate email messages whenever an event occurs, and the daily activity reports are sent to them daily to inform them about the events within the last 24 h. The typical format of the BSCW log files is as follows:

```
User:[3434841, '*******']
object:[3452718, 'Presenta**** A**** S*****']
Type:RateEvent
Time:1078202945.04
Members:[[3448332, '******', 'OyvLkYg2ueStI '],
        [3449370, '*****',
        ... ,
        [3425007, 'Aula 5 (*****)'],
        [3425034, 'Espai ***************'],
        [3425118, 'Espai Presentacions ']]
On:[3425118, 'Espai Presentacions ']
```

```
Touched:[3434844,  ':********']
Icon:'/bscw_resources/icons/e_write.gif'
Class:Document
Content:application/octet-stream
```

Note that user and group information have been anonymized.

The BSCW log does not follow a standard log format, hence, parsing these logs thus formatted requires a customized development. Moreover, relevant data are omitted, in the example above the student 3434841 is rating the resource 3452718 but there is no additional information, such as the rate value.

5.4.3 BASIC SUPPORT FOR COOPERATIVE WORK STUDENT COLLABORATIVE WORK INDICATORS

With the aim of accessing documents, meetings, and contacts in shared work spaces, users can also organize their collaboration via tasks and the coordination of meetings. Blogs, forums, and Wikis are available for sharing information and documenting project results. BSCW users can share many objects, such as documents, notes, folders, blogs, etc. most of which can be rated in terms of qualification. Therefore we select the most usual objects in collaborative learning that can be rated, namely notes (posts on forums) and collaborative documents. An assessment of the document's quality may be provided by selecting one of the ratings offered by the LMS, though these ratings are not configurable and they follow the typical Likert scale (ie, good, fair, etc.).

Besides ratings, we collect general activity of students in the LMS. BSCW offers several methods and sources to obtain this user activity data. Among these methods, Web and mail activity reports, which can be configured manually only, cannot allow us to automatize the process. Moreover, if the LMS usage indicators need to be extracted in a normalized format, the manual methods do not allow this operation to be performed.

Dealing with these limitations, a rating and LMS general usage data collection model is needed, and so the BSCW API service has been studied to extend additional data which may be collected.

The global indicators generated by the BSCW that we considered for our data analysis are shown in Table 5.1.

Although the main information about X-BSCW is available in [185], the development of *BSCW-data-collector* has only been possible by means of the additional API specification and the BSCW API clients which are available in the documentation resources for developers [186].

In addition to global indicators, *BSCW-data-collector* can be configured to dump a subset of attributes. The results are available in extensible markup language (XML) format, thus the output of the dump process may be stored in several formats, such as comma separated values (CSV), name-value, printable, etc. Finally, the query that the client application sends can be customized using conditions, filters, offsets, and blocks of results.

Table 5.1 Global Indicators Generated by the BSCW

Indicator	Description
items	Number of items created in BSCW by the student S
items_null	Number of items created by S which cannot be rated
items_dynamic	Number of dynamic items (ie, forum posts) created by S
items_static	Number of static items (ie, document) created by S
ratings_static	Number of ratings, in static items created by S
ratings_static_by	Number of ratings performed by S in static items
ratings_dynamic	Number of ratings, in dynamic items created by S
ratings_dynamic_by	Number of ratings performed by S in dynamic items
sum_ratings_static	The sum of the rating value for each rating, in static items created by S
sum_ratings_static_by	The sum of the rating value for each rating, in dynamic items created by S
sum_ratings_dynamic	The sum of the rating value for each rating, in dynamic items created by S
sum_ratings_dynamic_by	The sum of the rating value for each rating performed by S in dynamic items

Note: BSCW indicators are calculated for each student (S) in a collaborative work group.

5.4.4 PARALLELIZING BASIC SUPPORT FOR COOPERATIVE WORK LOG FILE PROCESSING

We examined BSCW API parallelizing options with the aim of speeding up processing.

Basically we measured *BSCW-data-collector* speed up and efficiency for different executions of the following parameters:

1. number of items requested;
2. parameter configuration, that is, number of parameters per item;
3. filters and conditions, for instance, only documents created by a student S; and
4. size of blocks and offsets in responses.

Fig. 5.3 shows *BSCW-data-collector* benchmark results representing the time taken in processing the request (in ms) for a certain number of items requested. For instance, if we request 1 item to BSCW, the time spent by the server is 3956 ms and if we request 900 items, elapsed time is 4106. This test is executed with the following cases:

1. *Basic ratings*: Basic data such as for ratings are retrieved from the LMS and the output format only contains elemental values.
2. *Basic request*: Basic general data is returned for each element (ie, name, description, creator, etc.) and the results are stored in a CSV format.
3. *Complex request*: We collect the whole set of attributes of each item and the output contains text lines with the attribute name and its value.

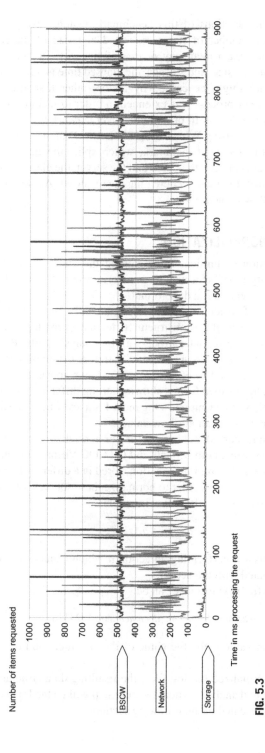

FIG. 5.3

Basic support for cooperative work API benchmark results.

Even with several variations of this benchmark, results have shown a similar behavior, namely, the number of items requested, the size of the result and the storage format do not experiment any degree of linearity. In other words, for a different number of items, size, and storage, the elapsed time is fixed. Our hypothesis was that this behavior might be caused by factors other than those considered. Therefore the benchmark process was extended in order to include additional tasks involving *BSCW-data-collector*. In order to discover network times in each request, we measured these values using Wireshark [187] network analysis tool.

Fig. 5.4 shows the second benchmark, which splits the time spent into: the communication process between the client and the server, the elapsed time in storage tasks, and the time spent by the server creating the result set. As shown in the figure, the results do not follow a linear model.

5.4.5 LOG FILE NORMALIZATION

Log data normalization or unification is gaining the attention of the autonomic computing community [188] as a way to transform proprietary and heterogeneous formatted log data to standard log data format.

In [116], the task of structuring event log data can be defined as the processes which provide structure to the semistructured textual event log data and persist the resulting data structure for later processing by analysis tools. Real e-Learning scenarios are usually formed by several LMS. Therefore the input of the process is a set of LMS log files generated by each source. As shown above, every log file, such as BSCW and UOC, has its own format showing strong differences in the formatting styles (eg, in the UOC Virtual Campus a log record is a text line in the text file whilst in BSCW each line represents an attribute value).

Moreover, we cannot consider either unifying or normalizing those logs generated by the same Web Server (eg, both Moodle and the UOC Virtual Campus use Apache Web Server, but they log different information stored in a different format). Hence, a preliminary process is needed in order to normalize these sources following a unified format. To this end, we propose the following tuple:

$$L = (u, t, a, [v] *), \tag{5.2}$$

which represents a user u performing an action a which occurs in time t. A list of values $[v] *$ is associated with the action.

An example of a $(a, [v]*)$ instance can be:

$$(create\_document, \ document.txt, \ 1024\,kb), \tag{5.3}$$

where the first action-value is the file name of the document and the second is the size of the document.

Once we have normalized the log files, the resulting data structure persists for later data processing and analysis. Then, the next step will be the log data processing approach, which is presented in the following sections.

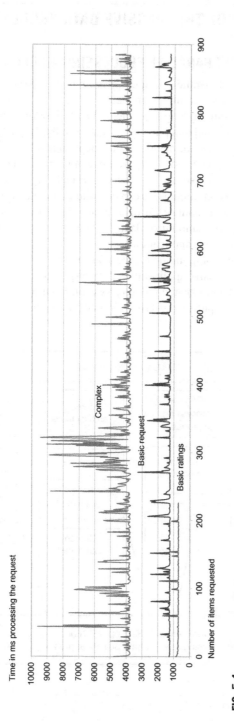

FIG. 5.4

Basic support for cooperative work API benchmark-components.

5.5 APPLICATION OF THE MASSIVE DATA PROCESSING APPROACH

5.5.1 SELECTING THE PARALLEL PROCESSING MODEL

From the classification of parallel computing presented in Section 5.1, Fig. 5.5 highlights the categories selected for our model.

Regarding the programming language, the software development process takes into account decomposition and mapping issues related to the *Map* and *Reduce* tasks. Although these considerations are mandatory for deployment factors, the rules that we have followed in the process of software development are natively supported by Hadoop. For this reason, we actually select the category *everything implicit*. Therefore parallelism and communication considerations are totally implicit and thus the Hadoop framework will manage all operations related to communication and parallelism. Due to the large amount of data, P2P student activity data processing was considered a data-intensive application.

Although we need data computation for the analysis process, the processing tasks do not require compute-intensive applications. With respect to memory architectures, we propose a distributed and isolated memory system. Each node manages its own memory space and the output of the task is stored in the distributed file system.

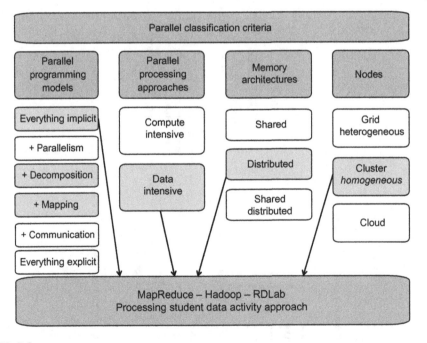

FIG. 5.5

Parallel classification criteria.

Finally, we propose a homogeneous cluster architecture with identical nodes. The main reason for selecting this architecture is the nature of the case, that is, we are dealing with a data-intensive application.

5.5.2 APPLICATION TO LOG FILE ANALYSIS

The main software applications developed address the processing of the log file records (ie, log file lines), through a classification process that extract the useful information for student activity data analysis. These applications are based on a study of the types of records registered in the Open University of Catalonia (UOC) Virtual Campus log files. The core of the service is implemented in a Java class *Action*, which offers the main methods to process a record. An action object represents something which occurred in the UOC Virtual Campus servers.

The main services and methods offered by the class *Action* (see Fig. 5.5) are a set of get methods (eg, *get_date()*, *get_ip()*, *get_junk()*, etc.) intended to parse each log line. The following classification summarizes the output records, which are managed using each corresponding method:

- *Record (R)*: It represents a log file line.
- *Invalid record (IR)*: An IR is a record, which does not have a valid key. A valid key is a tuple with these components: session, IP, and time.
- *Valid record (VR)*: In contrast, a VR contains each necessary field to form a valid record key.
- *Request record (RR)*: This type of record is a VR, which has a valid request (ie, the server generated a 200 return code value).
- *Short record (SR)*: If a VR does not meet conditions of RR (ie, request and 200 code).
- *Junk record (JR)*: We define a JR as a RR that does not contain relevant data.
- *Analysis record (AR)*: We select such records that are relevant to a specific analysis as AR.
- *System record (SR)*: Since the set of AR is selected for a specific case study, there are a certain quantity of RR which are not considered in the analysis. We refer to these records as System Records.

Fig. 5.6 shows the inheritance records relationships.

5.5.3 MAPREDUCE LOG FILE PROCESSING

The parallel implementation in the distributed infrastructures that we propose in this section follows the MapReduce paradigm (see Section 5.3.1). Therefore we first introduce our MapReduce model on the normalization of different LMS log files, namely BSCW and UOC, described in previous sections. The results obtained will be used to conduct our parallel implementation approach based on Hadoop and cluster computing presented in the following sections.

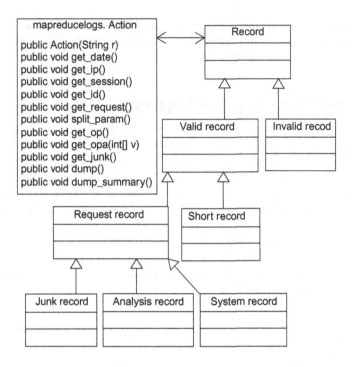

FIG. 5.6

Apache log records and action class diagram.

In our real learning context of the UOC, the complexity of the e-Learning tasks entails the utilization of multiple LMS. For this reason, the target student activity data of our proposal is a set of LMS log files generated by each system (see Fig. 5.7). Each log file has its own format, in our case, BSCW [181] and UOC Virtual Campus log formats are completely different. Even considering the logs generated by the same Web Server, each server uses different formats. Hence, we can assume that each log file type is a semistructured text file with record-oriented structure, and the input data set is made up of many files storing log information (eg, each LMS, log per day, etc.). The input may be represented as:

$$I = \log_{l}^{i}, \quad l \in L, \ i \in I, \tag{5.4}$$

where L is the set of LMS, and I is the set of log files in an LMS.

The MapReduce paradigm works by splitting the processing into two stages, the *Map* phase and the *Reduce* phase, and each phase has key-value pairs as input and output. Therefore we define the tasks in the *Map* phase and those processed in the reduce phase, selecting the input and output keys for each phase. In this paradigm, the output from the map function could be processed by the framework before being sent to the reduce function.

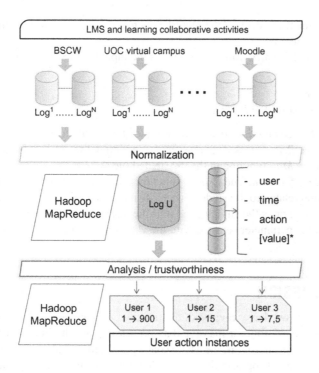

FIG. 5.7

Log file normalization architecture for MapReduce parallel computing.

The *Map* Phase

The *Map* phase takes as input a record stored in a log file in I. The key of this record is the offset in the file. When the *Map* function receives the record, it will be processed following the normalization process which was presented above, and this output will be the input for the *Reduce* function. At this point, we can decide between several alternatives dealing with the reduce function. In order to only store normalized data, the reduce task does not perform additional work and store the output of the map function in the distributed file system. In addition, the reduce function may be used to compute a relevant component as presented in the previous section. In that case, one of the keys is the student and the reduce function calculates the result of the parameter selected (eg, number of documents created by the student, total session time, sum of ratings, etc.).

To sum up, we have proposed a normalization architecture (see Fig. 5.7) based on a parallel MapReduce approach as follows:

- The *Map* phase takes a record stored in a log file.
- The *Map* key of this record is the offset in the file.

- The *Map* function receives the record, which is processed following the normalization process.
- The output of the *Map* function is sent as the input for the *Reduce* function.

Reduce Phase

Two options exist for the *Reduce* phase:

- *Without Reduce function*: If we only want to store normalized data for further analysis, the *Reduce* task does not perform additional work, it only stores the output of the *Map* function in the distributed file system.
- *With Reduce function*: The *Reduce* function is used to compute relevant information related to the student's activity data. One of the keys computed by the *Map* function is the student, and thus the *Reduce* function aggregates the results of the parameter selected with the aim of modeling the student's task.

5.6 DISCUSSION

In this chapter we have reviewed the most commonplace parallel computing paradigms and platforms for massive data processing. While there is a plethora of parallel computing paradigms, the MapReduce paradigm is shown as most suitable to massive processing of log data files, given that the data split, mapping, and reducing phases can be efficiently implemented. Additionally, the integration of MapReduce with Apache Hadoop greatly simplifies the implementation and deployment in a real Hadoop cluster. Therefore the MapReduce Hadoop is the choice when dealing with the massive processing of log data files.

It should be noted that in the context of trustworthy approaches, the implementation of parallel approaches arises due to the need to process large amounts of collaborative learning data, which is in fact the basis for building effective trustworthy profiles.

Trustworthiness evaluation and prediction

6

6.1 e-LEARNING CONTEXT

6.1.1 REAL ONLINE COURSE FEATURES

In order to evaluate the trustworthiness and security approach proposed in this book, experimental activities were conducted in three real online courses in our real learning context of the Open University of Catalonia (UOC). For all the three real cases, which are implemented at UOC, we have selected a sample of groups for the sake of the data analysis and presentation of the results. The methodology is the same for scaling it up to other e-Learning courses at UOC.

In the first study (hereafter *CSCL-course-1*) student evaluation was based on a hybrid CA model by using manual and automatic e-Assessment instruments. Twelve students were distributed in three groups and the course was arranged in four stages. These stages were taken as time references in order to implement trustworthiness sequences. At the end of each stage, each student had to complete a survey. The coordinator also had to complete two reports, namely public and private ones, thus evaluating the members of the group. In the former report, the group coordinator releases a public report evaluating the individual and group performance, while the latter report is not disclosed to group members; only the course instructor has access to that report. The details of the CSCL-course-1 study are presented in Section 6.1.2.

The second study (hereafter *P2P-course*) was designed for evaluating a massive deployment for automatic e-Assessment processes. The course was focused on Peer-to-Peer e-Assessment developed by 57 students performing a P2P e-Assessment, that is, each student was requested to assess the rest of their class peers in terms of knowledge acquired and participation in the class assignments. The course followed seven stages, according to a software development plan, which were taken as time references in trustworthiness analysis. In this course, we implemented a hybrid e-Assessment approach by combining manual and automatic e-Assessment methods, and the model enabled us to compare results in both cases. The details of the *CSCL-course-1* are presented in Section 6.1.3.

Intelligent Data Analysis for e-Learning. http://dx.doi.org/10.1016/B978-0-12-804535-0.00006-X

Finally, the third study (hereafter, *CSCL-course-2*) followed the same design as *CSCL-course-1*. However, we incorporated the enhancements detected during the first study.

6.1.2 COLLABORATIVE ASSESSMENT COURSE

In the first study (*CSCL-course-1*), student evaluation was based on a hybrid CA model by using manual and automatic assessment instruments. The experiment focused on a real online course at the Open University of Catalonia with the following features:

- Collaborative activities represent a relevant component of the pedagogical model of the course. The student evaluation process is based on a CA by using several manual evaluation instruments.
- 12 students, distributed in four groups, participated in the experience.
- The course followed four stages (t_1, t_2, t_3, t_4) taken as time references in order to evaluate and analyze the results. These stages corresponded to a software development process.
- At the end of each stage t_i, all students completed a questionnaire (Q_1, Q_2, Q_3, Q_4). These questionnaires refer to the set Q defined in the trustworthiness model.
- Each stage was performed in collaborative working groups and was coordinated by a different member of the group in a rotating fashion, namely, every student plays the coordinator role during a stage. The coordinator of the group completed two reports (ie, the set RP in the model, namely, public $\overline{RP}$ and private RP), at the end of each stage evaluating the members of the group:

$$\left(\overline{RP}_1, \overline{RP}_2, \overline{RP}_3, \overline{RP}_4, RP_1, RP_2, RP_3, RP_4 \right).$$

- General e-Learning activities were supported by a standard LMS, whose tools supported both rating (ie, the set RT in the model) and general learning management indicators (LI).

Once we tracked the problem of large amounts of ill-structured data in LMS log files with a MapReduce approach, as mentioned in the course features above, we worked with a sample of logs generated by the activity of 12 students.

Note that questionnaires, reports, and learning management indicators were defined regarding trustworthiness data sources, indicators and levels in Chapter 3. Next, we summarize several general features related to the aforementioned research instruments:

- *Ratings*: Qualifications of objects in relation to assessments, which can be rated or qualified by students in the LMS.
- *Questionnaires*: Instruments that allow us to both collect student trustworthiness information and to discover general design aspects in our model.

- *Student reports*: Assessment instrument containing questions and ratings performed by the students and reviewed by the tutors.
- *LMS usage indicators*: To collect students' general activity in LMS.

6.1.3 PEER-TO-PEER ASSESSMENT COURSE

The second case study (*P2P-course*) was aimed at building and deploying our comprehensive e-Assessment methodology. The key features of the course can be summarized as follows:

- Student e-Assessment was based on a manual CA model by using several manual e-Assessment instruments.
- Manual e-Assessment was complemented with automatic methods, which represented up to 20% of the student's total overall grade.
- Taking into account several features, we implemented a hybrid e-Assessment method by combining manual and automatic e-Assessment methods to compare results in both cases.
- 59 students performed a P2P e-Assessment, that is, each student was requested to assess the rest of their class peers in terms of knowledge acquired and participation in the class assignments.
- The course followed seven stages, which were taken as time references in trustworthiness analysis. These time references were used to compare trustworthiness evolution as well as to carry out e-Assessment methods.
- Each stage corresponded to a module of the course, which had a learning component that the student should have studied before carrying out the assessment activities of the course.

From the above methodology, we designed the P2P e-Assessment component, which is presented in the following sections.

Finally, for the sake of simplicity, we called the continuous assessment P2P e-Assessment component, continuous assessment (CA).

6.2 TRUSTWORTHINESS EVALUATION

6.2.1 BUILDING COLLABORATIVE COMPONENTS WITH TRUSTWORTHINESS AND SECURITY METHODOLOGY

After the experience of designing the components in the first study, we built a comprehensive P2P assessment component in the second one. We selected integrity and identity as target security properties for the component and, after the analysis of student interactions in learning activities, a first version of the P2P assessment component was built. The component comprised three activities: in the first one, once the student had studied a module, the student received an invitation to a survey (*S1*) with questions about that module. The second activity of the component was a student forum (F), which created a collaborative framework devoted to enhancing response quality in $S1$. Eventually, the student had to complete another survey ($S2$), which contained the set of responses from the first one ($S1$). By using $S2$, the student had to evaluate the responses of each classmate as well as the participation of each student in the forum F. The design of this activity endorsed our proposal regarding the analysis of security properties, student interactions, and factors.

Regarding research instruments for data collection, we included the following:

1. surveys,
2. ratings,
3. student reports, and
4. LMS indicators.

To sum up, each instrument was integrated into the collaborative activity and managed its own data formats.

6.2.2 NOTATION AND TERMINOLOGY

Before the analysis and data processing phase, we recall here the key terms presented in the following sections (see Table 6.1). This table contains several items also considered in Chapter 3 as well as some additional notations, which were used for the evaluation process.

6.2.3 ANALYSIS AND DATA PROCESSING WITH TRUSTWORTHINESS AND SECURITY METHODOLOGY

We analyzed research instrument data formats in terms of data sources in trustworthiness and security methodology (TSM). For each case, we selected a set of normalization functions intended to convert basic trustworthiness data into normalized trustworthiness values.

Normalization functions are combined with trustworthiness levels and indicators (see Fig. 6.1). As a result of this combination, when a student evaluates the responses of each classmate, we use the following normalization function:

$$N\left(tw_{R_{q,m,s}}\right) = \sum_{j=1}^{N_S} \frac{tw_{R_{q,m,j}}}{N_S - 1}, \quad j \neq s, \, N_S = |S|, \, q \in Q, \, m \in M, \, s \in S, \, j \in S, \quad (6.1)$$

where $tw_{R_{q,m,s}}$ is the responses (R) indicator, s is the target student (ie, the student evaluated), N_S is the number of students in the course, and q is one of the questions evaluated in the module m.

With respect to normalized trustworthiness levels Ltw^N, we managed the composition of several indicators. The most suitable level in both courses is based on a weighted model:

Table 6.1 Notation and Terminology in Trustworthiness Evaluation Processes

tw_i	Trustworthiness indicator tw_i
$i \in I$	Set of trustworthiness indicators
N_I	Number of trustworthiness indicators
$m \in M$	Module m in the set of modules M
N_M	Number of modules
$q \in Q$	Question q in the set of questions Q
N_Q	Number of questions
$s \in S$	Student s in the set of students S
N_S	Number of students
CA	CA component
DS_{ca}	CA data sources, $ca \in \{R, F, Q_r, Q_c\}$
DS_{Q_r}	Questionnaire DS for the students' responses
DS_{Q_c}	Questionnaire DS for the number of responses
DS_R	P2P questionnaire DS for the score that a student has given a student's response
DS_F	Forum participation DS for the number of posts
$N()$	Normalization function
w_i	The component normalization weight for the indicator tw_i, $w_i \in (w_1, \ldots, w_n)$
$N_2()$	Normalization function for responses data source DS_R
$N_4()$	Normalization function for forum participation data source DS_F
$tw_{ca_{q,m,s}}$	Trustworthiness indicator for the CA component
$tw^N_{ca_{q,m,s}}$	Normalized trustworthiness indicator for the CA component
$tw_{R_{q,m,s}}$	Trustworthiness indicator for the students' responses score data source DS_R
$tw_{F,m,s}$	Trustworthiness indicator for the forum participation
L^N_I	Generic normalized trustworthiness level
$L^N_{R,m,s}$	Normalized trustworthiness level for students' responses
$L^N_{F,m,s}$	Normalized trustworthiness level for forum participation
$L^N_{m,s}$	The overall normalized trustworthiness level
$CATS_s$	CA trustworthiness sequence (CATS) ordered list
$CATS$	CATS matrix
$CATS^a_s$	Active CA trustworthiness history sequence
$CATS^c_s$	Constrictive trustworthy history
$CATS^W_s$	Trustworthiness window sequence

$$Ltw^N = \sum_{i=1}^{N_I} \frac{tw_i \cdot w_i}{N_I}, \quad i \in I, \ w_i \in (w_1, \ldots, w_{N_I}), \ \sum_{i=1}^{N_I} w_i = 1, N_I = |I|, \qquad (6.2)$$

where N_I is the total number of trustworthiness indicators and w_i is the weight for the normalized indicator tw_i.

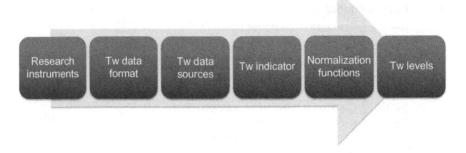

FIG. 6.1

Trustworthiness levels and indicators.

In order to process data, we analyzed both sequential and parallel data processing implementations. Sequential approaches were feasible for managing data sources from several activities, such as responses in a survey or number of posts in a forum. However, processing the log data took too long to complete and it had to be done offline (ie, after the completion of the learning activity). For this reason, we endowed our trustworthiness framework with parallel data processing. To this end, we designed a MapReduce algorithm implemented in an Apache Hadoop [117] and deployed it in the RDlab [189] high-performance computing cluster. Using this model, a considerable speed up was achieved in processing large log files, namely, more than 75% for 10 nodes (see Section 7.2 for further details).

6.2.4 ASSESSMENT, PREDICTION, AND EVALUATION WITH TRUSTWORTHINESS AND SECURITY METHODOLOGY

Peer-to-Peer components were designed considering the time factor. Activities were arranged in stages that led to the definition of trustworthiness sequences. In both studies, trustworthiness indicators and levels were noted at several points in time (eg, the same indicator measured for each module) and arranged in trustworthiness sequences. The concept of trustworthiness sequence in an e-Assessment component allowed us to support assessment and prediction. Actually, it could be directly incorporated, in some cases, as input for assessment and prediction methods. Regarding validation, we experimented with a hybrid validation approach by combining manual, automatic, external, and internal validation methods. In this model, we analyzed the similarity between manual evaluation results and automatic trustworthiness levels. The proposed method to measure the similarity was based on Pearson correlation [98].

Finally, we considered two different methods to deal with trustworthiness prediction. The first approach was based on NNs [82] and the second one on collaborative filtering. On the one hand, a NN captures any type of nonlinear relationship between input and output. In our case, the input was the trustworthiness history sequence and the output was the prediction calculated by the neural network (ie, predicted trustworthiness value). On the other hand, filtering recommendation algorithms concern the prediction of the target user's assessment, for the target item that the user has not given the rating, based on the user's ratings on observed items. In our context, the items involved in the recommendation system were the students themselves.

In the rest of this chapter, we focus the validation of TSM on trustworthiness prediction based on a NN approach. TDS, indicators, normalization processes, and history sequences are also applied.

6.2.5 TRUSTWORTHINESS DATA SOURCES, LEVELS, AND INDICATORS

We first describe the TDSs, indicators and levels in the context of our CA. Recall that a trustworthiness data source is data generated by the CA that we used to describe the trustworthiness features presented in Chapter 3. Each CA (ie, one CA per module) will manage four data sources.

The first is related to the students' responses and can be denoted with the following ordered tuple:

$$DS_{Q_C} = (M, Q, S, count),\qquad(6.3)$$

where the questionnaire data source is the total number of responses (*count*) that each student in S has answered in the questionnaire Q for the module M.

The second data source also refers to the students' responses and the DS offers each specific response:

$$DS_{Q_R} = (M, Q, S, res),\qquad(6.4)$$

where the questionnaire data source DS_{Q_R} is the response res (ie, a student answers res to a question) that each student in S has responded regarding a specific question in Q in the module M.

The third data source refers to the participation degree in a forum. These data sources can be denoted with the following ordered tuple:

$$DS_F = (M, F, S, count),\qquad(6.5)$$

where the forum data source DS_F is the total number of posts (*count*) that each student in S has sent to a forum F regarding a specific question in Q in the module M.

Finally, we introduce a score data source as follows:

$$DS_R = (M, Q, S, SS, score),\qquad(6.6)$$

where the response data source denotes the score that a student (in S) has given a student's (in SS) response to a question in Q. Hence, S is the set of students who assess and SS is the set of students who are assessed by students in S. Although S

and SS may be considered as the same set of students in certain applications, they are actually considered as different sets because we permit participation in the second stage of the activity even when the student has not carried out the first one.

Tuples in DS_R are stored in a relational database table, namely MySQL [190].

Once TDSs have been applied, we select three trustworthiness levels. Following the model defined in Chapter 3, we first combine the trustworthiness indicators of each question in the module, and then the overall trustworthiness level for the student in a specific module is:

$$L_{R,m,s} = \sum_{i=1}^{n} \frac{(tw_i \cdot w_i)}{n}, \quad i \in Q, \; w = (w_i = w_j), \; m \in M, \tag{6.7}$$

where $L_{R,m,s}$ is the trustworthiness level for the student s in the module m measured by the trustworthiness indicator tw_i, which considers the responses for each question in Q.

$$L_{F,m,s} = tw_{F,m}, \quad m \in M, \tag{6.8}$$

where $tw_{F,m}$ is the trustworthiness indicator for the responses in the collaborative forum F for the module m.

$$L_{m_i s} = \sum_{i=1}^{n} \frac{Ltw_i \cdot w_i}{n}, \quad i \in \{L_{R,m}, L_{F,m}\}, \; w = (w_i = w_j), \; m \in M, \tag{6.9}$$

where $L_{m_i s}$ is the overall trustworthiness level for the student s in the module m, calculated by combining the trustworthiness level for responses $L_{R,m,s}$ and the trustworthiness level for forum participation $L_{F,m,s}$.

6.2.6 STATISTICAL ANALYSIS AND INTERPRETATION

Here we analyze the trustworthiness levels and indicators presented in the previous section. The graph presented in Fig. 6.2 shows the overall $L_{R,m,s}$ for each student and for each module. It is worth mentioning that students who had not participated in any CA activity have been omitted. In this graph the $L_{R,m,s}$ level for each student has been accumulated by module, as shown in Fig. 6.2.

Regarding student participation, we monitored participation values (see Fig. 6.3) revealing a decrease of participation level after considering the following information:

- Q: Questionnaire participation.
- F: Total number of posts in the forum.
- FP: Participation in the forum.
- P: P2P survey participation.

In contrast to the decrease in the participation level, with respect to the evolution of the overall scores in the course, these values were steady across all the modules

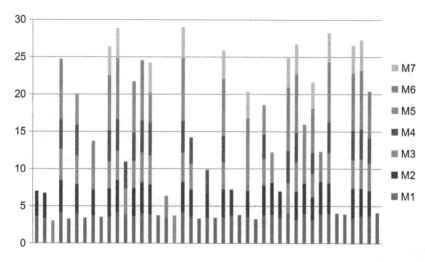

FIG. 6.2

$L_{R,m,s}$ level for each student and module.

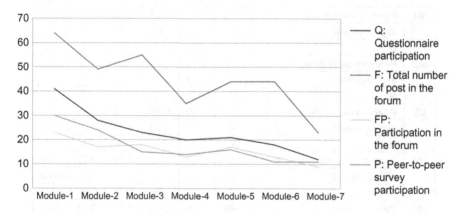

FIG. 6.3

Student participation evolution.

in the course. The overall scores evolution is shown in Fig. 6.4, which presents the overall score result for each module activity, that is, $L_{R,m,s}$ and $L_{F,m,s}$ without considering the values for each specific student and detailing each question for $L_{R,m,s}$ (ie, $Q1$, $Q2$, and $Q3$).

We calculated the correlation coefficient between the values corresponding to the time references 1–7 (ie, each module in the course). The results of the correlation analysis are shown in Fig. 6.5. Pearson's correlation is close to 1 for most of the cases, hence a strong relationship is found between trustworthiness levels in modules.

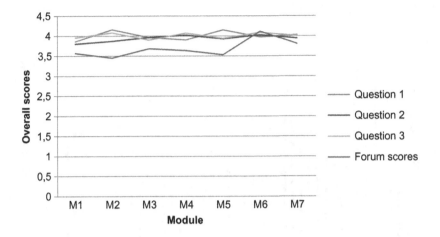

FIG. 6.4

Overall scores in the course.

		M1	M2	M3	M4	M5	M6	M7
M1	Pearson correlation	1.00	**0.70**	0.64	0.54	0.59	0.54	0.63
	sig. (2-tailed)		0.00	0.00	0.01	0.01	0.02	0.03
	N	40	26	22	20	20	18	12
M2	Pearson correlation	0.70	1.00	**0.89**	0.81	0.86	0.81	0.69
	sig. (2-tailed)	0.00		0.00	0.00	0.00	0.00	0.02
	N	26	26	20	18	19	16	11
M3	Pearson correlation	0.64	0.89	1.00	**0.83**	0.76	0.80	0.79
	sig. (2-tailed)	0.00	0.00		0.00	0.00	0.00	0.00
	N	22	20	23	19	18	16	12
M4	Pearson correlation	0.54	0.81	0.83	1.00	**0.78**	0.76	0.80
	sig. (2-tailed)	0.01	0.00	0.00		0.00	0.00	0.00
	N	20	18	19	20	16	15	11
M5	Pearson correlation	0.59	0.86	0.76	0.78	1.00	**0.75**	0.90
	sig. (2-tailed)	0.01	0.00	0.00	0.00		0.00	0.00
	N	20	19	18	16	21	16	11
M6	Pearson correlation	0.54	0.81	0.80	0.76	0.75	1.00	**0.86**
	sig. (2-tailed)	0.02	0.00	0.00	0.00	0.00		0.00
	N	18	16	16	15	16	18	12
M7	Pearson correlation	0.63	0.69	0.79	0.80	0.90	0.86	1.00
	sig. (2-tailed)	0.03	0.02	0.00	0.00	0.00	0.00	
	N	12	11	12	11	11	12	12

FIG. 6.5

Pearson coefficient between trustworthiness levels in modules.

The observed correlation is positive, consequently, when the trustworthiness level increases in module i, trustworthiness level in module $i + x$ also increases in value. The *sig.* value is less than 0.05, hence we can conclude that there is a statistically significant correlation between trustworthiness levels. Note that in Fig. 6.5 we have marked those values that correspond to correlation between consecutive modules (ie, $r_{m_i, m_{i+1}}$), in these cases, the coefficient is always more than 0.7.

Finally, in order to compare manual and automatic assessment results, a prior step is needed. We organized both manual and P2P activities in a timeline diagram with the aim of comparing manual and automatic activities in suitable time references (see Fig. 6.6). To this end, we designed a course plan that permits the comparison

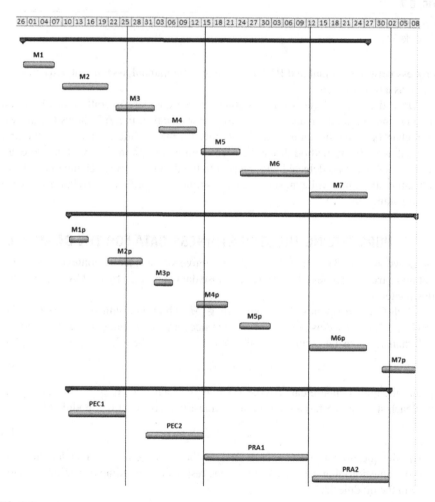

FIG. 6.6

Timeline diagram for manual and P2P assessment activities.

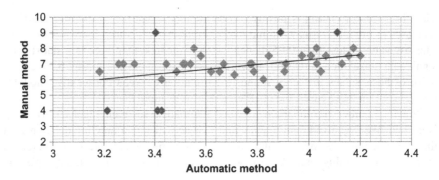

FIG. 6.7

Dispersion chart between the automatic P2P and manual assessment methods for module 1.

process between manual and P2P assessment. The manual assessment activities are taken as a time reference.

Once the time references are established, we compare overall values between manual and automatic assessment methods. For instance, Fig. 6.7 shows the dispersion chart between the automatic P2P activity for the module 1 (ie, R_1) and the first manual assessment method. It can be seen from the graph in Fig. 6.7 that there are few anomalous cases detected with respect to the difference between the manual and the automatic value, while most of the values follow a significant correlation between these parameters.

6.2.7 NORMALIZING TRUSTWORTHINESS DATA FOR THE CA MODEL

Next, we analyze TDSs and levels. In the university academic context of CA, we defined a trustworthiness data source as those data generated by the CA as presented in Chapter 3.

Each CA corresponds to a module $m \in M$, which is a unit of the course. The modules will be used as point in time references. Each CA (ie, one CA per module) will manage three data sources, which are denoted with the following ordered tuples:

$$DS_{Q_C} = (M, Q, S, count), \qquad (6.10)$$

where the questionnaire data source DS_{Q_C} is the total number of responses (*count*) that each student in S has answered in the questionnaire Q for the module M.

$$DS_{Q_R} = (M, Q, S, res), \qquad (6.11)$$

where the questionnaire data source DS_{Q_R} is the response *res* (ie, a student answers *res* to a question) that each student in S has responded regarding a specific question in Q in the module M.

$$DS_F = (M, F, S, count), \qquad (6.12)$$

where the forum participation data source DS_F is the total number of posts (*count*) that each student in S sent to a forum F regarding a specific question in Q in the module M.

$$DS_R = (M, Q, S, SS, score),\qquad(6.13)$$

where the response data source denotes the score that a student (in S) has given a student's (in SS) response to a question in Q. Hence, S is the set of students who assess and SS is the set of students who are assessed by students in S.

In this case, modeling trustworthiness involves multiple complex and heterogeneous data sources with different formatting, which cannot be managed without normalization. According to the model presented in Chapter 3, we apply the normalized trustworthiness indicator for the case of a CA as follows:

$$tw_{ca_{q,m,s}}^N = N\left(tw_{ca_{q,m,s}}\right),\quad ca \in DS_{R,F,Q_r,Q_c},\ q \in Q,\ m \in M,\ s \in S,\qquad(6.14)$$

where DS_{R,F,Q_r,Q_c} are the CA data sources, S is the set of students, M is the set of modules, and Q is the set of questions in each module.

We now apply the normalization functions. Note that although in Chapter 3 we included four normalization functions, in this case, a subset is selected: N_2 and N_4. The reason for this is that we focus the data analysis on two data sources, forum participation (N_4) and questionnaires (N_2). Regarding the response data source R, a student can assess the responses of each classmate. To this end, we use the normalization function N_2:

$$N_2\left(tw_{R_{q,m,s}}\right) = \sum_{i=1}^{N_S} \frac{tw_{R_{q,m,i}}}{N_S - 1},\quad i \neq s,\qquad(6.15)$$

where $tw_{R_{q,m,s}}$ is the response indicator, s is the target student (ie, the student who is assessed), N_S is the number of students in the course, and q is one of the questions assessed in the module m.

It should be noted that the scale for $tw_{R_{q,m,s}}$ must be converted to integer values before normalizing with function N_2. Similarly, the forum participation indicator also needs normalization. In this case, we apply the normalization function N_4:

$$N_4\left(tw_{F,m,s}\right) = \frac{tw_{F,m,s}}{T_F},\quad m \in M, s \in S,\qquad(6.16)$$

where T_F is the maximum number of posts in the forum by a student s in the module m.

6.2.8 BUILDING A P2P e-ASSESSMENT WITH TRUSTWORTHINESS AND SECURITY METHODOLOGY

The e-Assessment component is formed by the following three assessment activities and procedures:

1. After completing the study of a module M, the student received a request to answer a set of questions about that module. This is the first activity of the e-Assessment component named the module questionnaire and denoted by Q.
2. The second activity of the e-Assessment is a student forum F intended to create a collaborative task devoted to enhancing responses in activity Q. The forum activity F is performed in the UOC Virtual Campus.
3. The final activity is the core of the P2P assessment and the student has to complete a P2P assessment survey P, which contains the set of responses from Q. The student has to assess each peer response in Q and, furthermore, the activity of each student in the forum F is assessed.

Algorithm 1 presents the formulation of the algorithm corresponding to the above e-Assessment process of the CA.

ALGORITHM 1 ALGORITHM FOR THE e-ASSESSMENT PROCESS

Require: M {the list of modules} and S {the set of students in the course}

```
 1: for m: M do
 2:     Qm ← create_questionnaire(m)
 3:     send(Qm, S)
 4:     Fm ← create_forum(m)
 5:     F(m) ← class_discussion(Fm, S)
 6:     Q(m) ← getResponses(Qm, S)
 7:     Pm ← create_P2P_eval(Q(m), S)
 8:     send(Pm)
 9:     P(m) ← getResponses(Pm, S)
10:     e_assessment(m)[] ← results(Q, F, P, S)
11: end for
12: return e_assessment(m)[]
```

6.2.9 ANALYSIS OF THE RESULTS

In this section we summarize the most relevant findings from the results and the statistical analysis.

The results of the P2P (ie, automatic) and continuous (ie, manual) assessment over all levels reveal a significant difference between the overall range of these values. Fig. 6.7 shows that most of P2P assessment values are in the range from 3.5 to 4.3 (according to the e-Assessment scale from 1 to 5) and the CA, from 1 to 9 (on a 0 to 10 scale).

Although the scales were from 1 to 5 and 0 to 10, the student assessment results are in the ranges [3.2; 4.4] and [3.2; 4.4]. Fig. 6.8 shows the same result as Fig. 6.7, but considering the complete range of allowed values.

The results of the comparisons between manual and automatic assessment showed that:

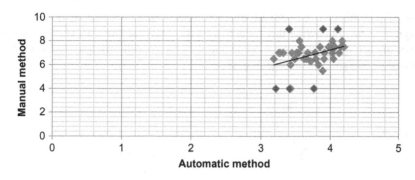

FIG. 6.8

Dispersion chart between the automatic P2P and manual assessment methods for module 1 (complete range of values).

- The mean difference between manual and automatic methods is 0.81 (the scale used from 0 to 10).
- The maximum and minimum difference: 0.03 and 2.82.
- The percentage of assessment cases in which the difference between manual and automatic assessment is less than 1 (ie, 10% with respect to the maximum score) is about 76.92%.
- If we extend the difference to more than 2 points between manual and automatic assessment, the percentage of assessment cases in this range is 92.31%.

The most significant finding is related to some cases of Anomalous User Assessment, namely, students for which the assessment results were not conclusive and required further investigation in order to prevent authenticity flaws in the student assessment results. Indeed, three students whose deviation is greater than 20% were found and were considered anomalous in terms of correct classification. Their assessment required further investigation for potential cheating in order to validate the authenticity (ie, identification and integrity) of their corresponding learning outcomes.

6.3 TRUSTWORTHINESS PREDICTION

6.3.1 TRUSTWORTHINESS LEVELS AND SEQUENCES

In Section 6.2.7 we normalized the trustworthiness indicators for forum participation and responses (ie, a student answers a question in the questionnaire). Additionally, in this section, trustworthiness levels are used to measure overall trustworthiness of students. To this end, we considered the following trustworthiness levels:

$$L_I^N = \sum_{i=1}^{N_I} \frac{\left(tw_i^N * w_i\right)}{N_I}, \quad i \in I, \ w_i \in (w_1, \ldots, w_{N_1}), \ \sum_{i=1}^{N_I} w_i = 1, \qquad (6.17)$$

where N_I is the total number of trustworthiness indicators and w_i is the weight assigned to tw_i. Following this model, we first combined the trustworthiness indicators of each question in the module and thus the overall trustworthiness level for the student in a specific module $m \in M$ is:

$$L_{R,m,s}^{N} = \sum_{q=1}^{N_Q} \frac{\left(tw_q^{N} * w_q\right)}{N_Q}, \quad q \in Q, \ N_Q = |Q|, \tag{6.18}$$

$$\sum_{q=1}^{N_Q} w_q = 1, \quad w_q = \frac{1}{N_Q}, \ m \in M, \ s \in S, \tag{6.19}$$

$$L_{F,m,s}^{N} = N_4\left(tw_{F,m,s}\right), \quad m \in M, \ s \in S, \tag{6.20}$$

$$L_{m,s}^{N} = \sum_{j=1}^{2} \frac{\left(Ltw_j^{N} * w_j\right)}{2}, \quad j \in \left\{L_{F,m}^{N}, L_{R,m}^{N}\right\}, \tag{6.21}$$

$$\sum_{j=1}^{2} w_j = 1, \quad w = (0.4, 0.6), \ m \in M, \ s \in S, \tag{6.22}$$

where $L_{m,s}^{N}$ is the overall trustworthiness level for the student s in the module m, calculated by combining the trustworthiness level for responses $L_{R,m,s}^{N}$ and the trustworthiness level for forum participation $L_{F,m,s}^{N}$.

After selecting the trustworthiness levels, we consider time factor for our model. Although the concept of trustworthiness sequence was proposed in the context of grid services and requesters [101], it is feasible to apply this approach to another modeling scenario, such as P2P e-Assessment. The only requirement is time factor, in other words, the model should allow us to compute an overall trustworthiness level referred to multiple points in time. Therefore we define CA trustworthiness sequence CATS as the ordered list of a student's trustworthiness history levels over several points in time:

$$CATS_s = \left(L_{m_1,s}^{N}, \ldots, L_{m_k,s}^{N}, \ldots, L_{m_{N_M},s}^{N}\right) m_k \in M, \quad s \in S, \tag{6.23}$$

where M is the set of modules, each module m_k refers to a point in time and $L_{m_k,s}^{N}$ is the overall trustworthiness level for the student s in the module m_k.

Likewise, we can define the overall student CA trustworthiness history sequence as the matrix:

$$CATS = \begin{pmatrix} L_{m_1,s_1}^{N} & \cdots & L_{m_1,s_{N_S}}^{N} \\ \vdots & \ddots & \vdots \\ L_{m_{N_M},s_1}^{N} & \cdots & L_{m_{N_M},s_{N_S}}^{N} \end{pmatrix}, \tag{6.24}$$

where N_M is the number of modules (ie, points in time analyzed), and N_S is the number of students in the course.

6.3.2 TRUSTWORTHINESS SEQUENCE RESULTS

Processing trustworthiness sequences results involves large amounts of data generated by the P2P activity of the CA. To this end, we compute the following elements:

1. The trustworthiness history sequence matrix has $N_S * N_M, N_S = |S|, N_M = |M|$ elements.
2. For each element in *CATS*, $L_{m,s}^N$, we compute both forum participation and response trustworthiness levels.
3. Forum participation is a single indicator with three different questions.
4. For each trustworthiness level we compute each student's score for the indicator.

   With the aim of managing these trustworthiness sequence results, we developed a data parse *Java* tool called *parse_tw_tuples* that converts P2P values into the basic tuples presented above. This tool generates basic tuples from the Web applications, and these primitive records can be imported in a relational database for further processing. As the size of the results might be a relevant issue, we consider the size of the resulting set of records generated by each data source. At the end of the process the responses data source maximum size is:

$$|DS_R| = |M| \times (|Q| + 1) \times |S| \times |S|, \tag{6.25}$$

where $|M|$ is the number of modules, $|Q|$ is the number of questions (+1 is added because the student also assesses the forum activity), and $|S|$ is the number of students who could participate in both questionnaires (ie, Q and P).

   To sum up, the diagram depicted in Fig. 6.9 shows the overall process including how we need to normalize data sources. Thus this figure shows the creation of trustworthiness indicators and levels, and finally, the procedure presented to compose trustworthiness sequences.

6.3.3 PREDICTING WITH TRUSTWORTHINESS SEQUENCES

So far, we have presented the design of trustworthiness history sequences in the P2P e-Assessment components of the target online course. To this end, we considered the main concepts presented in [101] related to trustworthiness history sequences as a foremost step in trustworthiness prediction based on NN design.

   Active trustworthiness history sequence is the recent trustworthy history sequence. Thus, we define active CA trustworthiness history sequence $CATS_s^a$ as the ordered list of student trustworthiness levels over the points in time:

$$CATS_s = \left(L_{m_1,s}^N, \dots, L_{m_k,s}^N, \dots, L_{m_{N_M},s}^N \right), m_k \in M, s \in S \tag{6.26}$$

$$CATS_s^a = \left(L_{m_{N_Q-a+1},s}^N, L_{m_{N_Q-a+2},s}^N, \dots, L_{m_{N_M},s}^N \right), s \in S, \tag{6.27}$$

where M is the set of modules, each module m_k refers to a point in time, and $L_{m_k,s}^N$ is the overall trustworthiness level for the student s in each module.

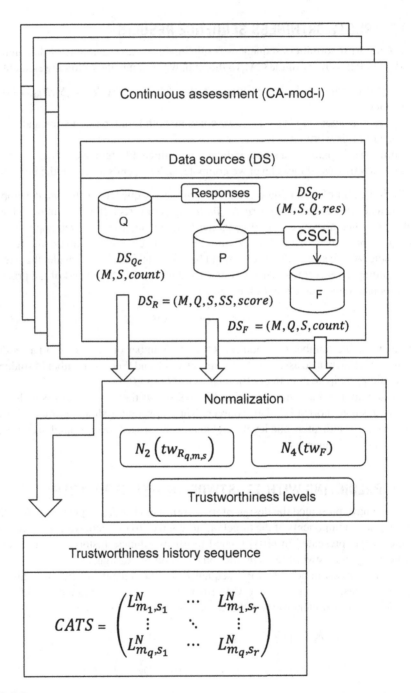

FIG. 6.9

CA data sources, normalization, and trustworthiness sequences.

Constrictive trustworthy history is the subsection average of active trustworthy history sequence.

$$CATS_s^c = \left(L_{m_{1...N_S},s}^N, L_{m_{r+1...N_Q},s}^N, \dots \right), s \in S, \tag{6.28}$$

where each element in the tuple is the average of a subset of elements in $CATS_s^a$, and k is the number of inputs of NN.

These tuples are presented in order to prepare those input sets that are required in NN training and validation. The concept of trustworthiness sequences in prediction with NN is also suggested in [82]. In this proposal, the trustworthiness sequence is split into subsequences of fixed sizes, without average transformation:

$$CATS_s^W = \left(L_{m_1,s}^N, \dots, L_{m_w,s}^N \right), \left(L_{m_{w+1},s}^N, \dots, L_{m_{2w},s}^N \right), \dots, s \in S, \tag{6.29}$$

where each component in the trustworthiness window is a subset of the $CATS_s$.

6.3.4 NN e-ASSESSMENT

Among existing models of trustworthiness-based prediction, we selected the NN-based approaches for predicting trust values presented in [82,101], because these approaches are feasible in the context of e-Assessment. Although these models present several significant differences between each other, especially with respect to how to build training sets, these differences are also considered in our e-Assessment proposal. In the rest of the chapter, we incorporate our NN model into a training set based on $CATS_s^W$. We consider this approach more suitable for our case because $CATS_s^W$ generates a greater amount of training sequences.

A NN can capture any type of nonlinear relationship between input and output data through iterative training. In our case, the input is the CA trustworthiness history sequence formed by trustworthiness results generated by the P2P assessment component, and the output is the prediction calculated by the NN (ie, trustworthiness predicted value):

$$L_{m_{t+1},s}^N = NN\left(CATS_s \right), s \in S, \tag{6.30}$$

where entity s denotes the student whose normalized trustworthiness level value is being predicted through the $CATS_s$ representing data generated by the P2P activity of the CA, and m_{t+1} denotes the trustworthiness point in time in the future predicted by the function NN for the student s (ie, the output of the NN).

As presented in [82], the main principle of neural computing is the decomposition of the input-output relationship into a series of linearly separable steps using hidden layers. The NN architecture (see Fig. 6.10) is composed of sets of neurons that are arranged in multiple layers. The first layer, whose inputs are fed into the network, is called the input layer.

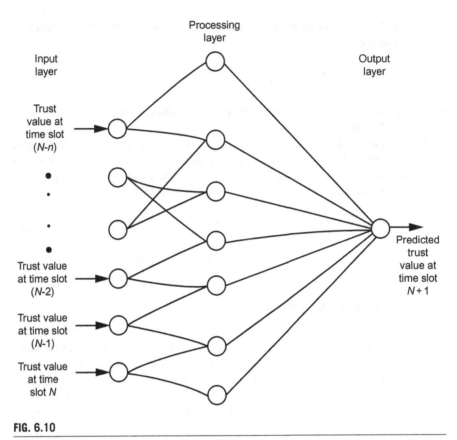

FIG. 6.10

A simple NN approach for trust prediction [82].

The last layer, which produces the NN output, is called the output layer. The layers in between these two layers (ie, between input and output layers) are all hidden layers. The input consists of values that constitute the inputs for the hidden layers.

Every node computes a weighted function of its inputs and applies an activation function to compute the next output. The output is transmitted to all the connected nodes on the next layer with associated weights. The activation of each node depends on the bias of the node, which calculates the output as follows:

$$y_j = \sum_{i=0}^{n} w_{ij} x_i, \tag{6.31}$$

where y is the result of the sum of each input x multiplied by its associated interconnection weight w. The initial weights are assigned randomly but they are gradually changed to reduce the error. The difference between the desired output and the actual output constitutes the input to the back propagation algorithm for training the network based on the difference.

Through the iterative training, the NN produces better prediction accuracy in the domain of time series prediction, such as trustworthiness history sequences.

6.3.5 THE "EMERGENT" SOFTWARE TOOL AND ANALYSIS OF RESULTS

With the aim of implementing the NN for trustworthiness prediction, we evaluated several Neural Network simulators. Among them, we selected *Emergent* [191] as a suitable software tool that meets all the requirements for our case. *Emergent* (formerly PDP++) is defined as a comprehensive, full-featured deep neural network simulator that enables the creation and analysis of complex, sophisticated models [192]. The main reasons for using *Emergent* in the context of this chapter can be summarized as follows:

- *Emergent* provides powerful visualization and infrastructure tools.
- It provides a structured environment for using and modifying models based on NN templates, as well as test and training programs.
- *Emergent* is completely open source software.
- Highly optimized run-time performance. In fact, we deployed the simulator environment in a virtual machine running on a personal computer.

With the aim of developing a first simulation approach in *Emergent*, we carried out the following tasks:

1. A new simulation project was created based on the template BpStd (ie, standard initialization of back-propagation). This resource is provided by *Emergent* and allows the designer to begin the NN design from a standard configuration.
2. We generated and configured a standard network, specifying number of layers, layer names, sizes, types, and connectivity. The NN is formed by 3 layers with 2 input values and 1 output. In terms of *Emergent* design, the geometry for both input and hidden layers is a 2 unit x 1 unit matrix.
3. The NN geometry corresponds to the size of the data contained in the *StdInputData* table. This table contains each student's trustworthiness window sequence $CATS_s^W$ defined in Section 6.3.1. The data import process was managed through text file elements (see Fig. 6.11). *Emergent* offers import and export tools that bind the *StdInputData* tables and the text files.
4. Once NN basic design and input data were configured, the next step was the training process of the NN. Following the model defined in Section 6.3.3, we split the input values for each student into two trustworthiness sequences (ie, training and test). The training trustworthiness window sequence contained 5 instances (ie, time slots or modules in the course), which were arranged in tuples of 3 elements. The 3-tuple was also divided into the input values and the output

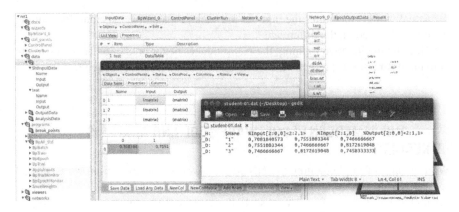

FIG. 6.11

Snapshot of network *StdInputData* and text files.

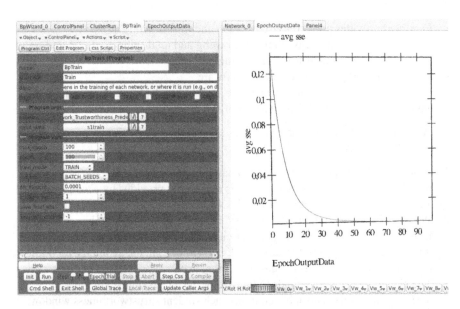

FIG. 6.12

Training process parameters and simulation.

result. Therefore for each $CATS_s^W$ sequence we generate tuples of 3 elements containing the 2 input values and the expected output value.

5. The training process was managed by *Emergent* in the *BpTrain* program whose initial parameters are shown in Fig. 6.12.

6. Finally, we introduced the test elements in order to validate the model.

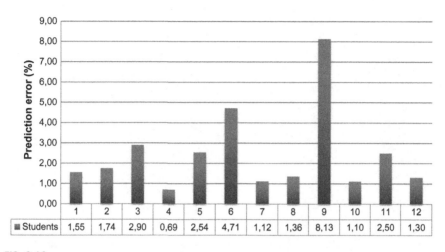

FIG. 6.13

Students NN prediction results.

The deviation in prediction results for each student is depicted in Fig. 6.13. The sample of the experiment was formed by 12 students. Fig. 6.13 presents the results obtained from the NN simulation process for each student. The horizontal axis represents students and the vertical axis represents the difference between the value predicted by the NN and the test value (ie, the prediction error in absolute value). For instance, the NN for the student five predicted a value with 2.54% of error.

Interestingly, the results on the overall error prediction reveal a significant similarity between the test and predicted values, but we cannot demonstrate the stability of this prediction approach for other cases (ie, more differences in trustworthiness evolution).

With respect to e-Assessment security (ie, e-Assessment authenticity), the most significant finding is related to detection of anomalous user assessment cases. From these data, two students (see students 6 and 9 in Fig. 6.13), whose error prediction is greater than 3%, were found to be anomalous and required further investigation for identifying potential cheating in order to validate the authenticity of the student learning activity.

Finally, we found that the number of modules in the course (ie, the slots or the reference time points) must be increased to achieve more accurate prediction. Indeed, if the number of training instances is increased, the student's NN is able to accurately predict a greater number of different trustworthiness values (not only those cases with low variation in trustworthiness evolution).

Trustworthiness in action: Data collection, processing, and visualization methods for real online courses

7

7.1 DATA COLLECTION AND PROCESSING METHODS

For the analysis of the data collected during the *CSCL-course-1* study, we used a parallel processing approach, which considerably decreased the time of data processing, thus allowing for building relevant trustworthiness models to support learning activities even in real time. During the data collection phase, we managed two different formats of log files, namely, the BSCW and Learning Management System of the UOC Virtual Campus.

Before providing some parallel implementation details, we first show the different formats of BSCW [181] and UOC (Web-based virtual campus of the UOC) log files. Due to different formats, we first dealt with the large size and ill-structured information found in the considered log files. To handle this problem, a normalization approach for both types of log data was proposed as an input to our general parallel model as $L = (u, t, a, [v] *)$, which represents user u performing an action a, occurring in time t. In addition, a list of values $[v] *$ is associated with the action.

The parallel implementation is based on the MapReduce paradigm. Therefore we implemented a MapReduce model on the normalization of different LMS log files. The deployment of the parallel implementation is done using Hadoop and the cluster computing approach presented in Chapter 5. This computational model showed that a considerable speedup is achieved in processing large quantities of log file data.

7.1.1 TRUSTWORTHINESS DATA PROCESSING

As mentioned earlier, the Peer-to-Peer e-Assessment in the questionnaire P produced a great amount of output data. These data are stored in a relational MySQL database as follows:

Intelligent Data Analysis for e-Learning. http://dx.doi.org/10.1016/B978-0-12-804535-0.00007-1

$$P2P = (M, Q, S, SS, score), \tag{7.1}$$

where P2P denotes the score that a student has given a student's response of a question in Q. Hence, S is the set of students who assess and SS is the set of students who are assessed by students in S.

To guarantee student privacy and protect the e-Assessment results, we created an additional table, which stores a random integer value for each student. This random value is assigned to every student; hence, the data stored for each P2P tuple are not linked to the identity of the student. In other words, student assessment information remains anonymous when we export the students' results to external systems.

Note that the maximum size of P2P e-Assessment responses is computed as follows:

$$max\{P2P\} = |M| \times (|Q| + 1) \times |S| \times |S|, \tag{7.2}$$

where $|M|$ is the number of modules, $|Q|$ is the number of questions (+1 is added because the student assesses the forum activity and the questions in the questionnaire Q), and $|S|$ is the number of students who could participate in both questionnaires (ie, Q and P).

The total number of computed tuples representing student P2P assessment instances for the experiment *P2P-course* was:

$$|P2P| = 10.522 \tag{7.3}$$

Finally, Fig. 7.1 shows a sample set of data extracted from the P2P e-Assessment results and the number of results per module.

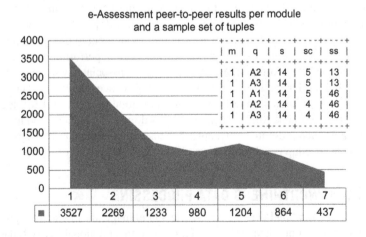

e-Assessment peer-to-peer results per module and a sample set of tuples

m	q	s	sc	ss
1	A2	14	5	13
1	A3	14	5	13
1	A1	14	5	46
1	A2	14	4	46
1	A3	14	4	46

	1	2	3	4	5	6	7
■	3527	2269	1233	980	1204	864	437

FIG. 7.1

Trustworthiness data processing overall results.

7.1.2 RESEARCH INSTRUMENTS AND TECHNOLOGICAL TOOLS

For the purpose of the e-Assessment component implementation and deployment, we used Web survey services, export and import tools, parse applications, and data conversion developments. The e-Assessment component is summarized in the rest of this section.

To implement and deploy a CA, a questionnaire creation function was developed (ie, *create_questionnaire*, see Algorithm 1). Since the output of the first questionnaire (see variable $Q(m)$ in the algorithm) is the input to the P2P assessment activity (ie, variable P_m), we could automate the assessment process for each CA. This function was implemented as a Java class named *CreateP2P*, which included the set of attributes and methods required to automatically generate the assessment activity P_m. The automation capabilities of the process are actually focused on the set of responses and the survey P_m manual customization, such as the text or the invitation messages.

The CA used two Web survey applications. The module questionnaire (Q) was implemented in Google Forms [193] and the P2P questionnaire (P) with LimeSurvey [194]. Due to the data exchange requirements between the two survey tools, we selected the Comma Separated Values (CSVs) format as the data exchange model. For this reason and with the aim of simplifying the implementation process we integrated into our Java components the package Super CSV [195], which offers advanced CSV features dealing with reading and writing advanced operations on lists of strings.

In addition, we selected LimeSurvey because highly configurable export and import survey functions based on standard formats were needed. After the evaluation of several survey formats, we selected the CSV option. The function *create_P2P_eval* has been implemented by the Java class *create_P2P_csv*, which receives a CSV responses file containing the set of responses collected by Google Forms and creates a LimeSurvey CSV survey format by converting the responses into questions for the new P2P questionnaire. The hosting support for LimeSurvey framework was provided by the RDlab laboratory [189].

Moreover, because of the P2P and dynamic features of the questionnaire P, we needed to extract assessment results in primitive and normalized e-Assessment data format as presented in the following section. To this end, we developed the Java class *Results*.

Finally, to deal with processing the Pearson correlation coefficient, we used the statistical analysis program GNU PSPP [196].

The overall process of building the assessment component is depicted in Fig. 7.2.

7.2 MapReduce APPROACH IMPLEMENTATION

7.2.1 Hadoop DEVELOPMENT FRAMEWORK

We selected Cloudera CDH4 QuickStart VM [197] as the development environment for our MapReduce application. This virtual machine contains a standalone Apache Hadoop framework with everything we needed to test our model.

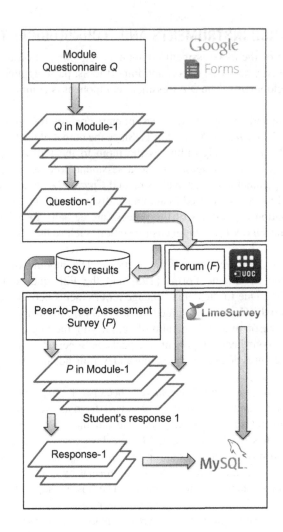

FIG. 7.2

The process of building the P2P e-Assessment component.

Moreover, this development framework is completely compatible with the real cluster in which the application was deployed. Although Cloudera CDH4 Quick-Start VM is an Apache Hadoop MapReduce preconfigured framework, we identified several configuration and management issues that were tailored to our case as follows:

1. *Integrated development environment (IDE) and Java libraries*: Although Cloudera CDH4 QuickStart VM includes Eclipse IDE [198], it may be harmful in terms of performance to use the same virtual machine for several purposes. To this end, we decided to import Hadoop and Java base libraries to an external

Netbeans IDE [199]. Both Eclispe and Netbeans IDEs are compatible with the Java binaries generated for the cluster framework.

2. *Distributed file system*: Once the MapReduce applications were developed, before testing and running the jobs in parallel processing, network and distributed file systems settings were required to load input and store results. Indeed, the distributed file systems configuration is a foremost step in parallel testing, which required system actions, such as user's home creation, configuration of the input directory for jobs, and upload process of the input files.

3. *Running Hadoop MapReduce jobs*: Although the compiling tasks were developed using the IDE framework facilities, Hadoop needs a Java archive (JAR) packet format as job application input. Hence, we compiled and built the set of applications in JAR format. Finally, we launched our Hadoop jobs by running the following commands:

```
hadoop fs —rm —r —skipTrash $DIR/output
hadoop jar uoclog.jar
[UOCLogDriverCountOp|UOCLogDriverClean]
    $DIR/input $DIR/output
```

4. *Results*: On the completion of jobs, we examined the Hadoop MapReduce results. From the different formats generated by Hadoop, we used sequential and text files:

```
hadoop fs —ls $DIR/output
hadoop fs —cat|get|text $DIR/... /part—0
```

7.2.2 IMPLEMENTATION IN Hadoop

Our MapReduce Java implementation was completely based on the class *Action*, which was presented earlier in this section. We developed two separate Java applications, the *UOCLogDriverClean* for normalizing UOC log files and the *UOCLogDriverCountOp* for computing aggregate data. We describe these two applications next.

The *UOCLogDriverClean* application normalizes UOC log files cleaning unnecessary data. Only records in the set AR are considered as outcome and the other ones are ignored. To improve computational performance, the algorithm progressively inspects each condition in a well-arranged way, that is, firstly the most restrictive and general condition (eg, *has_session*) and finally the most specific one (eg, *has_opa*). The following code summarizes the *Map* phase:

```
public static class UOCLogMapperClean extends
    MapReduceBase implements
    Mapper<LongWritable, Text, Text, Text> {
    @Override
public void map(
    LongWritable key, Text value,
```

```
         OutputCollector<Text, Text> output,
                      Reporter reporter)
   throws IOException {
String record = value.toString();
Action act = new Action(record);
if (!act.is_empty) {
  act.get_date ();
  if (act.has_date) {
    act.get_ip ();
    act.get_session ();
    if (act.has_session) {
      act.get_id ();
      act.get_request ();
      if (act.has_request) {
        act.split_param ();
        act.get_op ();
        if (act.has_op) {
          act.get_junk ();
          if (!act.is_junk) {
            act.get_opa ();
            if (act.has_opa) {
              output.collect(
                new Text(act.id),
                new Text(act.request ));
}}}}}}}}
```

As shown in the above Java code, the mapper receives as parameters a pair (key, value), where the key is automatically generated by Hadoop and the value is a line of a log file. The output is a different pair, where the key is the record id and the value is the request. It is important to note that, in this case, we do not use a *Reduce* function because no reducing tasks (ie, grouping, computing, etc.) are needed.

The *UOCLogDriverCountOp* has both *Map* and *Reduce* functions with the aim of computing aggregate data (ie, compute the sum of each action type). The *UOCLog-DriverCountOp Map* code is similar to *UOCLogDriverClean* implementation but, in this case, the output key-value for the type of value is defined as an integer to compute each instance:

```
private final static IntWritable one =
                   new IntWritable(1);
public void map(
   LongWritable key, Text value,
   OutputCollector<Text, IntWritable> output,
                   Reporter reporter)
   throws IOException {
String record = value.toString();
```

```
Action  act  =  new  Action(record);
if  (!act.is_empty)  {
  ...    // The same conditions as
  ...    // UOCLogDriverClean
  output.collect(new Text(act.opa),  one);
  ...
}}}
```

When the *Map* function generates each key-value, it is combined according to the key and processed by the *Reduce* function:

```
public void reduce(
    Text key,
    Iterator<IntWritable> values,
    OutputCollector<Text, IntWritable> output,
                    Reporter reporter)
    throws IOException {
  int sum = 0;
  while (values.hasNext()) {
    sum += values.next().get();
  }
  output.collect(key, new IntWritable(sum));
}}
```

Finally, the collected data were stored in the output directory, which was defined when the job was run.

7.2.3 DEPLOYMENT AT THE HIGH-PERFORMANCE COMPUTING RDlab CLUSTER

The cluster support for our MapReduce implementation was provided by the RDlab [189]. The RDlab is focused on promoting research and development of computing projects within the departments of the Technical University of Catalonia [200].

The aggregated hardware resources are 160 physical servers, 1000 CPU cores, and more than 3 Terabytes of RAM memory, 130 TB of disk space, and high speed network at 10 Gbit. The RDlab's cluster offers the possibility of executing a Hadoop environment. The cluster integrates a parallel work management queue system with HDFS directly integrated into the Lustre [201] file system [202].

7.2.4 PERFORMANCE EVALUATION

The quantity of each type of record was of particular relevance for our log processing model, due to the quantity of AR (useful records) extracted from the log.

We run four types of record benchmarks for 10, 100, 1.000, and 10.000 MB log files. Results of these tests are shown in Fig. 7.3.

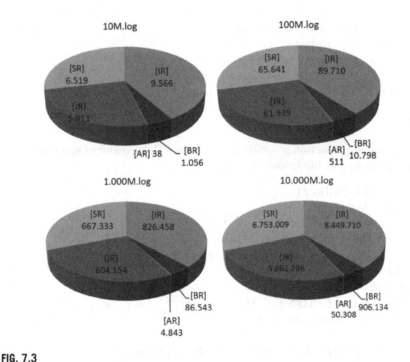

FIG. 7.3

Types of log record benchmarks.

We selected those records that were relevant to our specific analysis associated to the actions performed in the LMS that must be analyzed. Although we focus on student e-Learning and behavior actions, additional technological information, such as students' device or IP control, could also be included in the study. Tables 7.1 and 7.2 show the name of each action, a short description, and the number of user actions computed in each input log file.

7.2.5 ANALYSIS OF THE RESULTS

Once the MapReduce applications were developed, before running the jobs in parallel processing, network and distributed file systems were required. We use HDFS as a Hadoop MapReduce storage solution, therefore some file system configuration tasks were needed, such as creating user home file and defining suitable owner, creating MapReduce jobs input directory, uploading log files, and retrieving results actions (see Section 7.2.3).

Table 7.3 and the corresponding Fig. 7.4 show comparative results of the battery of tests with multiple Hadoop nodes (ie, 2, 4, 6, 8, and 10 workers) in RDlab [189] cluster. Note that the 0-node shows the results of the local sequential processing benchmark. Furthermore, we carried out additional file system integration processes

Table 7.1 The Actions Computed in Each Input Log File
1–500 MB

Name	Description	Benchmark (×MB)					
		1	10	50	250	100	500
Class	Access to a classroom	2	21	118	229	603	1112
In	Login LMS session	0	4	18	47	106	217
Out	Logout LMS session	1	2	3	8	17	23
File	Download a file	0	7	57	119	253	524
Mail	Load the email	0	0	1	3	11	37
Comm.	Community campus	0	0	3	9	22	55
Serv.	General services	0	0	1	7	19	38
Secr.	Secretary's office	0	2	13	33	69	127
Prof.	Load a user profile	0	1	7	12	22	40
News	UOC news service	0	1	7	14	28	41
Help	Help desk	0	0	1	2	6	11

Table 7.2 The Actions Computed in Each Input Log File
500–10,000 MB

Name	Description	Benchmark (×MB)				
		1000	2000	4000	8000	10,000
Class	Access to a classroom	2222	4429	8861	17,624	22,388
In	Login LMS session	461	904	1717	3623	4617
Out	Logout LMS session	67	155	325	747	954
File	Download a file	934	1982	4008	7841	9958
Mail	Load the email	118	232	466	835	973
Comm.	Community campus	123	263	536	1125	1390
Serv.	General services	66	126	273	521	642
Secr.	Secretary's office	295	648	1283	2563	3081
Prof.	Load a user profile	69	127	235	472	592
News	UOC news service	78	184	431	901	1087
Help	Help desk	20	49	127	264	316

by running Hadoop jobs over the open-source Lustre [201] file system, which is deployed in the RDlab.

From this experimental study, we can see that the results no longer grow linearly. We can also see that by using a distributed MapReduce Hadoop infrastructure, a considerable speedup was achieved in processing large log file data as shown in the last column of Table 7.3 (ie, more than 50% for infrastructures with more than 4 nodes and more than 75% for 10 nodes).

Table 7.3 MapReduce Results and Speedup (%) for 0–10 Nodes (N)

N	Log File Size											%
	1	10	50	250	100	500	1K	2K	4K	8K	10K	
0	0	0	2	2	9	19	35	75	141	288	353	
2	14	14	15	14	15	29	44	77	141	280	339	4
4	15	15	15	14	15	20	27	44	74	134	170	52
6	14	14	16	15	15	15	25	38	64	117	151	57
8	16	14	15	16	16	16	21	33	44	83	102	71
10	14	22	15	17	16	21	16	33	37	72	83	76

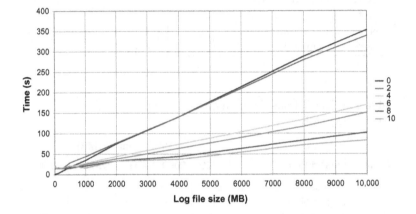

FIG. 7.4

Comparative MapReduce results.

On the other hand, for too small values of file size, the overhead introduced by the MapReduce framework was noticeable, as the framework control tasks spent too much time managing and distributing small amounts of data. In contrast, values for the task size close to 3000 MB considerably diminish this amount of time in comparison with the total processing time. Finally, we can see that reduce tasks perform poorly when the number of nodes is low.

7.3 PEER-TO-PEER DATA ANALYSIS AND VISUALIZATION

7.3.1 DATA ANALYSIS AND VISUALIZATION METHODS

From the visualization tools presented in Chapter 3, we evaluated several SNA applications. From the complete set of analyzed tools, we selected Cytoscape and Gephi. The selection of these tools was focused on the following features:

- The DS_R tuples were exported from the relational database to comma-separated value files. This file format was compatible with Cytoscape. However, Gephi offered a data edge list database connection and we directly connected to MySQL.
- Both tools offered a large set of layout models.
- Tutors could select multiple nodes (ie, multiple selection) and build the new graph with them.
- The edges corresponded to the e-Assessment relation between students in the P2P process.
- A score value assessed by each student was introduced by using an edge weight column. For this reason, the score value was also represented as an edge weight in the graph.

7.3.2 e-ASSESSMENT VISUALIZATION RESULTS WITH NodeXL

As presented in Chapter 3, NodeXL is an open source software tool especially designed to facilitate the learning of the concepts and methods of Social Network Analysis with visualization as a key component [144]. NodeXL works with Microsoft Excel and it is managed as a blank NodeXL template which shows the usual Microsoft Excel appearance and features.

The way we select to begin using NodeXL is to use the import command to load relationship data from an existing file or data source. Our data source is the CSV file containing all of the MySQL data set. Once data have been loaded into the template file, NodeXL offers several automatic layouts that can be selected from the control in the graph. The selected value used for our P2P e-Assessment model in the layout type for NodeXL is called Fruchterman-Reingold [203]. The *Fruchterman-Reingold* layout is a force-directed layout algorithm which treats edges like springs that move vertexes closer or further from each other in an attempt to find an equilibrium that minimizes the *energy* of the system.

7.3.3 e-ASSESSMENT VISUALIZATION RESULTS WITH Forcoa.NET

As introduced in Chapter 3, the Forcoa.NET system is built over the digital bibliography & library project (DBLP) data set [204] from the field of computer science [145]. The design and development of the system were driven by the requirement for the visualization of co-authorship data. A key requirement was the need for the visualization of an author and the author's surroundings in the context of their publication activities, including a simple animation for the visualization of historical data [145].

In the context of the P2P e-Assessment presented we can apply the Forcoa.NET system with the aim of visualizing P2P assessment interactions among the students. The visualization capabilities with respect to historical data are also related to e-Assessment processes, because trustworthiness (see Chapter 3) is closely related to time factor.

Moreover, time factor was included in the e-Assessment component implementation when students assessed their classmates throughout the sequence of seven modules in the course. Therefore Forcoa.net is a feasible visualization system for the P2P e-Assessment component described in this book.

Since the source format of Forcoa.NET was DBLP, we decided to adapt the e-Assessment results to a compatible DBLP format. Whereas student e-Assessment results are stored in a relational database, we can export these data to an XML template following the DBLP data set model.

The following schema allows us to extract the student's assessment information and to insert each value as a DBLP field:

```
<article  key="P2P-assessment-q1_s1_s2_m3"
          mdate="2015-01-01">
 <author>student 1</author>
 <author>student 2</author>
 <title>P2P assessment question 1</title>
 <pages>null</pages>
 <year>3</year>
 <volume>null</volume>
 <journal>null</journal>
 <number>4</number>
 <ee>null</ee>
 <url>null</url>
</article>
```

where the element *P2P-assessment-q1_s1_s2_m3* represents that *student 1* assessed *student 2* in *module 3*. The field title *P2P assessment question 1* is the assessed item (ie, the question in the questionnaire *Q*) and the field number 4 is the score (ie, scale of ratings) assigned by the *student 1*.

We evaluated several tools intended to convert relational database tuples to an XML specific model. For the sake of simplicity, we directly export e-Assessment results from MySQL.

```
SELECT
 CONCAT(
   '\n<article key="P2P-assessment-question-', q,
               '_student-', s,
               '_student-', ss,
               '_mod-', m, '">\n',
     '<author>student ', s,  '</author>\n',
     '<author>student ', ss, '</author>\n',
     '<title>P2P assessment question ', q, '</title>\n',
     '<pages>null</pages>\n'
```

```
        '<year>',  m,  '</year>\n',
        '<volume>null </volume>\n',
        '<journal >null </journal >\n',
        '<number>',  sc,  '</number>\n',
        '<ee>null </ee>\n',
        '<url >null </url >\n',
       '</article >\n'
   ) AS xmldoc
FROM scores_a;
```

Finally, those data generated by the above structured query language (SQL) statement are prepared and organized to import to the Forcoa.NET online service.

7.3.4 DISCUSSION

Even though we were not able to experiment in the online service of Forcoa.NET, we used NodeXL for performing visualization analysis tests. Although in NodeXL the default graph type is undirected (ie, the relationship between *student*1 and *student*2 is symmetric), we considered a directed relation, which represented that *student*1 assessed *student*2. As shown in Fig. 7.5, the tutor could select a student and the vertex for the students' e-Assessment relationships. When the tutor performed these actions, the edges in the graph appear as remarked edges (see Fig. 7.5). The remarked edges corresponded to the assessment relation between a student in the P2P process (ie, those students who assessed the selected student and the students who were assessed by the selected student). This graph allowed the tutor to discover general e-Assessment behaviors such as students who had a low number of P2P e-Assessments. Although these visualization tools only provide an overall view

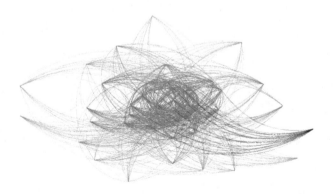

FIG. 7.5

The students' e-Assessment relationships.

Source: Created with NodeXL (http:// nodexl.codeplex.com).

FIG. 7.6

Weighted students' e-Assessment relationships.

Source: Created with NodeXL (http://nodexl.codeplex.com).

of the e-Assessment system, NodeXL also provides specific analysis views, that is, the tutors could select a subset of students. We also introduced the score value assessed by each student by using an edge weight column. For this reason, the score value is also represented as an edge weight in the graph (see Fig. 7.6). This type of column can be used to set visual properties of the edges as NodeXL uses automatic fill functions to set the edge width.

Conclusions and future research work

8

8.1 CONCLUSIONS AND LESSONS LEARNED

8.1.1 SECURITY IN COMPUTER-SUPPORTED COLLABORATIVE LEARNING

Throughout the book we have argued that current e-Learning systems supporting online collaborative learning do not sufficiently meet essential security requirements and this limitation can have a strong influence on the collaborative learning processes. To alleviate these problems we proposed an approach based on public key infrastructure (PKI) models that offer services which ensure essential security properties in online collaborative learning, such as availability, integrity, identification and authentication, access control, confidentiality, nonrepudiation, time stamping, audit service, and failure control. Finally, we justified that these technological measures alleviate security problems, but they cannot reach a comprehensive security solution for computer-supported collaborative learning (CSCL). The problems caused in online collaborative learning processes by the lack of security have been discussed and the main guidelines for the design of secure CSCL systems are proposed to guide developers in this domain to incorporate security as an essential requirement. We presented a first approach for designing secure LMS systems, whose central educational purpose is the provision and support of CSCL processes and activities, while security is the main and transversal requirement guiding the whole design process. To this end, we first provided background work in the context of LMS systems, CSCL, and main security services, such as PKI. Then, we provided general security services and requirements for e-Learning and specifically for CSCL. These approaches were finally merged to propose the main guidelines to design and develop secure collaborative learning management systems (SCLMS) that focus on the specific support for CSCL with security as a guiding requirement to conduct the whole design process. Through the exploitation of SCLMS in real contexts, it was proposed to enhance and improve the CSCL experience of all participants of the collaboration. An overview of secure LMSs was presented to inspect, the most relevant factors to consider and connect this approach to specific aspects for mobile

Intelligent Data Analysis for e-Learning. http://dx.doi.org/10.1016/B978-0-12-804535-0.00008-3

collaborative learning. Then, real-life experiences in security attacks in mobile learning were reported, showing a practical perspective of the vulnerabilities of the learning management system. From this experience and considerations, the main guidelines were proposed for the design of security solutions applied to improving mobile collaborative learning. Therefore this book proposed a first approach for designing secure mobile collaborative LMS. To this end, we proposed a model based on security properties, attacks, and PKI solutions by considering aspects related to CSCL and m-learning. The lack of provision of IS to MOOC was investigated with regard to anomalous user authentication, which cannot verify the actual student's identity to meet grading requirements well enough to satisfy accrediting institutions. In order to overcome this issue, a global user authentication model was proposed called MOOC smart identity agent (MOOC-SIA). This model included an innovative authentication process aimed at overcoming the anomalous student authentication issue in MOOCs, which is considered one of the most important barriers currently found in the MOOC arena. Furthermore, our model considered the massive nature of MOOCs and provides an authentication system flexible enough to meet each and every type of course and student profile. To this end, the MOOC-SIA model was designed to combine and set several authentication methods in MOOC platforms with the aim of offering a multifold solution combining different technologies, requirements, and user resources. To meet most of these requirements, we included a modular PKI-based security model as the main component that manages different authentication methods in the MOOC platform in a centralized fashion. Moreover, an innovative use of data mining techniques for education was considered in order to infer potential anomalous authentication from tracking MOOC participants.

8.1.2 TRUSTWORTHINESS METHODOLOGY

We proposed a methodological approach to modeling trustworthiness in online collaborative learning. This proposal aims at building a theoretical approach to provide e-Learning designers and managers with guidelines for incorporating security into online collaborative activities through trustworthiness evaluation and prediction. In this book, we first motivated the need to improve IS in online collaborative learning with trustworthiness solutions. Then, we proposed an innovative trustworthiness and security methodological approach to build secure CSCL activities and devoted to offering a comprehensive guideline for e-Learning designers and managers. Finally, the methodology was evaluated by presenting specific methods and techniques applied to real online courses. Moreover, we proposed a functional security model based on trustworthiness and collective intelligence. Both of these topics are closely related to online collaborative learning and e-Assessment models. Therefore the main goal of this book was to discover how security can be enhanced with trustworthiness in an online collaborative learning scenario through the study of the collective intelligence processes that occur in e-Assessment activities. To this end, a P2P student public profile model, based on trustworthiness is proposed, and the main collective intelligence processes involved in the collaborative e-Assessments activities were presented.

8.1.3 **TRUSTWORTHINESS EVALUATION AND PREDICTION**

An approach to enhance security in e-Assessment based on a normalized trustworthiness model was presented. In this book, justification is made of why trustworthiness normalization is needed and a normalized trustworthiness model is proposed by reviewing existing normalization procedures for trustworthiness applied to e-Assessments. To this end, we first motivated the need to improve IS in e-Learning and in particular in e-Assessment. Then, we showed the feasibility of building security hybrid models, based on trustworthiness approaches. However, trustworthiness analysis in e-Learning requires normalization processes to tackle several trustworthiness modeling problems presented in the book. As a main contribution of this book, we proposed a methodological approach for building a normalized trustworthiness model. Finally, we used a real online course intended to evaluate a hybrid evaluation system supported by our normalized trustworthiness model. The experimental results showed the feasibility of modeling security by analyzing normalized trustworthiness levels and indicators. From the results comparing manual evaluation and trustworthiness levels, it was inferred that it is viable to enhance security in e-Assessment by modeling and normalizing trustworthiness behaviors. In this book, previous trustworthiness models were endowed with prediction features by composing trustworthiness modeling and assessment, normalization methods, history sequences, and Neural Network-based approaches. To validate our approach, a P2P e-Assessment model was presented and carried out in a real online course. In particular, we presented an innovative prediction approach for trustworthiness behavior to enhance security in e-Assessment and this study showed how NN methods can support e-Assessment prediction. To this end, we first motivated the need to improve IS in e-Assessment with trustworthiness solutions based on time factor models in order to analyze prediction techniques. Then, we directed our research to P2P e-Assessment, and trustworthiness sequences with the aim of applying the concept of trustworthiness sequences customized for the P2P e-Assessment. Finally, we endowed our trustworthiness model with the prediction features by composing trustworthiness models, normalization, history sequences, and neural network models.

8.1.4 **DESIGN SECURE COMPUTER-SUPPORTED COLLABORATIVE e-ASSESSMENT**

A trustworthiness model for the design of secure collaborative learning e-Assessment in CSCL was proposed. In this book, we presented an innovative approach for modeling trustworthiness in the context of secure learning assessment in online collaborative learning groups. The study showed the need to propose a hybrid assessment model which combined technological security solutions and functional trustworthiness measures. This approach was based on trustworthiness factors, indicators, and levels that allowed us to discover how trustworthiness evolves into the learning system. We proposed several research instruments for collecting student data. Since extracting and structuring LMS data is a costly process, a parallel processing approach was proposed, which was fully developed and tested.

In addition, a trustworthiness-based approach for the design of secure learning activities in e-Learning groups was proposed by the presentation of guidelines of a holistic security model in online collaborative learning through an effective trustworthiness approach. To this end, we first motivated the need to improve IS in e-Learning and, in particular, in CSCL activities. Then, we proposed a methodological approach for building a security model for CSCL activities with the aim of enhancing standard technological security solutions with trustworthiness factors and rules. As a result, the guidelines of a holistic security model in online collaborative learning through an effective trustworthiness approach were first proposed. However, as learner trustworthiness analysis involves dealing with a large quantity of data generated during learning activities, processing this information is computationally costly, especially if required in real-time. To this end, and as a key contribution of this book, we developed and tested a parallel processing approach that can considerably decrease the data processing time, thus allowing for building relevant trustworthiness models to support learning activities even in real-time.

8.1.5 EXPERIMENTATION AND VALIDATION

Finally, in the last set of results and conclusions, we combined all the aspects under study, namely:

- definition of a security CSCL model,
- trustworthiness methodology,
- trustworthiness evaluation and prediction,
- design of secure CSCL activities and e-Assessment, and
- experimentation and validation.

We have carried out three studies in our real-life context of e-Learning of the UOC during the academic years of 2014 and 2015, with the aim of experimenting with specific trustworthiness and security approaches devoted to evaluating the feasibility of our trustworthiness models, tools, and methodologies. These studies are presented in the rest of this section and the key features of the pilots can be summarized as follows:

In the first study student evaluation was based on a hybrid continuous assessment (CA) model by using several manual and automatic assessment instruments. There were 12 students distributed in three groups and the course was arranged in four stages. These stages were taken as time references in order to implement trustworthiness sequences. At the end of each collaborative stage, each student had to complete a survey. The coordinator of the group had to complete two reports, public and private, and at the end of each stage, the members of the group were evaluated by the coordinator. General e-Learning activities were supported by UOC Virtual Campus Web-based services, while the collaborative activities were supported by the UOC's BSCW. BSCW is a fully web-based collaboration platform that facilitates efficient teamwork through a wide range of functions. The UOC's BSCW offered both rating systems and general learning management indicators.

The second study extended the scope of the first one to a more standard scenario. In this context, we were able to apply massive deployment for automatic e-Assessment processes. The course was focused on P2P e-Assessment and it has the following main features:

- Twelve students performed a subjective P2P e-Assessment, that is, each student was able to assess the rest of their class peers in terms of knowledge acquired and participation in the class assignments.
- The course followed seven stages which were taken as time references in trustworthiness analysis. These time references allow us to compare trustworthiness evolution as well as to carry out e-Assessment methods.
- Each stage corresponded to a module of the course, which had a learning component (ie, book) that the student should have studied before carrying out the assessment activities of the course.
- Student e-Assessment was based on a manual CA model by using several manual e-Assessment instruments.
- Manual e-Assessment was complemented with automatic methods, which represented up to 20% of the student's total overall course grade.
- Taking into account the previous features, we implemented a hybrid e-Assessment method by combining manual and automatic e-Assessment methods, and the model allowed us to compare results in both cases.

Finally, the third study followed the same design model as the first one. However, we incorporated the enhancements detected during the first development. We denote these courses as follows:

- *CSCL-course-1*: Hybrid assessment based on collaborative activities.
- *P2P-course*: Automatic P2P e-Assessment processes.
- *CSCL-course-2*: The second development of *CSCL-course-1* (the same design model as *CSCL-course-1*).

Moreover, the main outcomes related to experimental results are presented in the rest of this section following the next four topics:

1. Anomalous user assessment.
2. P2P visualization tools.
3. Trustworthiness prediction achievements.
4. Massive data processing.

Experimentation and validation: Anomalous user assessment

We proposed a trustworthiness model for the design of secure learning assessment in online Web collaborative learning groups. In this book, a holistic security model was designed, implemented, and evaluated in a real e-Learning context. Implications of this study were remarked upon for secure assessment in online collaborative learning through effective trustworthiness approaches. The study showed the need to propose a hybrid assessment model which combines technological security solutions and functional trustworthiness measures. To this end, a holistic security model was designed, implemented, and evaluated in a real e-Learning context. This approach is based on trustworthiness factors, indicators, and levels, which allowed us to discover how trustworthiness evolves into the learning system.

From the trustworthiness methodology, we designed the P2P e-Assessment component. The overall assessment model was a hybrid (ie, automatic and manual) approach formed by:

- *The peer-to-peer e-Assessment component*, which is automatic and the students were assessed by students.
- *The CA activities*, which is manual and the tutors assessed the students.

The results reveal a significant difference between the overall range of these values. Fig. 6.7 shows that most of P2P assessment values are in the range from 3.5 to 4.3 (the e-Assessment scale was from 1 to 5) and the CA, from 1 to 9.

The statistical analysis showed significant findings regarding the feasibility of the hybrid evaluation method. The results of the comparisons between manual and automatic e-Assessment indicate (also see Fig. 6.7):

- The mean difference between manual and automatic method is 0.81 (the scale used from 0 to 10).
- The maximum and minimum difference: 0.03 and 2.82.
- The percentage of assessment cases in which the difference between manual and automatic assessment is less than 1 (ie, 10% with respect to the maximum score) is 76.92%.
- If we extend the difference to more than 2 points on the scale, the percentage of assessment cases in this range is 92.31%.

The most significant finding was related to anomalous user assessment. From these data, three students whose deviation was greater than 20% were found to be anomalous and required further investigation for potential cheating in order to validate the authenticity (ie, identification and integrity) of their learning processes and results.

Experimentation and validation: Peer-to-peer visualization tools

We presented a P2P e-Assessment approach carried out in a real online course developed in our real e-Learning context of the Open University of Catalonia. The design presented in this book was conducted by our trustworthiness security methodology with the aim of building P2P collaborative activities, and then, enhancing e-Learning security requirements.

P2P visualization methods were proposed to manage e-Learning security events, as well as online visualization through P2P tools, intended to analyze collaborative relationships for monitoring the collaborative learning process by tutors and students.

The tutor can select a student and the vertex for the student e-Assessment relationships is remarked. The remarked edges correspond to the assessment relationship between a student in the P2P process; that is, those students who assessed the selected student; and the students who were assessed by the selected student. We also introduced the score value assessed by each student by using an edge weight column. For this reason, the score value is also represented as an edge weight in the graph.

Experimentation and validation: Prediction achievements

We proposed a methodological approach to modeling trustworthiness in online collaborative learning. Our proposal sets out to build a theoretical approach with the aim of providing e-Learning designers and managers with guidelines for incorporating security into online collaborative activities through trustworthiness evaluation and prediction. We proposed an innovative trustworthiness and security methodological approach for building secure collaborative activities devoted to offering a comprehensive guideline for e-Learning designers and managers. The architecture of the methodology was based on building trustworthiness learning components, trustworthiness analysis and data processing, and trustworthiness evaluation and prediction. The methodology was evaluated by presenting specific methods and techniques applied to real online courses.

We used two studies (*CSCL-course-1* and *P2P-course*), based on real online courses at the Open University of Catalonia, to evaluate and support the application and deployment of our trustworthiness methodology. Several significant aspects of our methodology were considered in terms of specific methods and techniques through their application in these real online courses. In the same study, we presented an innovative prediction approach for trustworthiness behavior to enhance security in e-Assessment. This study showed how NN methods may support e-Assessment prediction. These e-Assessment prediction methods were performed in a real online course based on P2P assessment processes and mobile online collaborative activities. The processes and learning activities involved in the course were encapsulated as CA components. Moreover, from this component, we presented the design of trustworthiness history sequences with the aim of designing an NN e-Assessment proposal.

The most relevant findings that emerge from the results presented were related to trustworthiness methodological applications and trustworthiness prediction models. Regarding the trustworthiness methodology proposed, we supported the application and deployment of the methodology in the real online courses presented (*CSCL-course-1* and *P2P-course*). The learning activities performed in the course were designed following the theoretical features, phases, data, and processes of our methodological approach.

With respect to trustworthiness prediction we focused the application of trustworthiness prediction on the course *P2P-course*. We demonstrated the feasibility of our NN prediction approach. Regarding the overall error prediction, the results revealed a significant similarity between the test and predicted values. From these results (see Fig. 6.13), we were able to detect anomalous user assessment. From these data, two students, whose error prediction is greater than 3%, were found to be anomalous and required further investigation.

Experimentation and validation: Massive data processing

The implementation of our parallel approach faced two important challenges: to handle several formats of log files coming from different LMS, and the large size of these log files. We showed how to normalize different log file structures as an input for the MapReduce paradigm to manage huge amounts of log data in order to extract the trustworthiness information defined in our model.

We used distributed infrastructure, Hadoop, and cluster computing, to implement and evaluate our parallelization approach for massive processing of log data. Experimental results showed the feasibility of coping with the problem of structuring and processing ill-formatted, heterogeneous, large log files to extract information on trustworthiness indicators and levels from learning groups and ultimately fill a global framework devoted to improving IS in e-Learning in real-time. We eventually concluded that it is viable to enhance security in CSCL activities by our trustworthiness model, though taking on the overhead caused by the use of distributed infrastructure for massive data processing.

Fig. 7.4 shows comparative results of the battery of tests with multiple Hadoop nodes (ie, 2, 4, 6, 8, and 10 workers). Note that the 0-node shows the results of the local sequential processing benchmark. From this experimental study, we can see that the results no longer grew linearly. By using a distributed MapReduce Hadoop infrastructure, a considerable speed up is achieved in processing large log file data as shown in Fig. 7.4. Regarding log file size, on the one hand, for too small values, the overhead introduced by the MapReduce framework when sending the parts to the nodes and combining output data is noticeable. Also, the framework control tasks spend too much time managing and distributing data. On the other hand, values of the task size close to 3000 MB considerably diminished this amount of time in comparison with the total processing time.

8.2 CHALLENGES AND FUTURE RESEARCH WORK

As ongoing work, the methodology testing and evaluation can be continued by deploying collaborative learning e-Assessment components in additional real online courses. Although the first pilot was developed in two academic years, we detected potential improvements for the second online course. For this reason, considering a sequence of courses in a row during an academic year would be beneficial to the study.

Since further deployments would require a large amount of data analysis, we propose to enhance the parallel processing methods presented in this book with the aim of managing trustworthiness factors and indicators. These enhancements can be achieved through improving the MapReduce configuration strategies that would result in improvement of a parallel speed-up, such as customized size of partitions.

Moreover, interesting steps in trustworthiness prediction methods can focus on evaluation and test processes. With respect to our prediction approach, to predict both student trustworthiness behavior and evaluation alerts (eg, anomalous results), we suggest evaluating additional NNs approaches and data mining models.

The next steps regarding the prediction model would involve investigating the usefulness of location-based information of mobile learners to our approach, with the purpose of improving trustworthiness evaluation and then, trustworthiness prediction. In addition, we discovered that the number of training instances should be increased. Therefore with the aim of enhancing the prediction model, we suggest modifying the learning activity presented in this study to generate more training instances. Hence, the student's NN would be able to more accurately predict a greater number of different trustworthiness cases (not only those cases with low variation in trustworthiness evolution).

In addition, an interesting ongoing project could be to implement e-Assessment solutions based on the proposed methodology that will extend the set of security properties considered as requirements, such as, privacy, nonrepudiation, and so on (ie, such as identity and integrity, which were selected as the most significant security properties in the scope of e-Assessment processes). To this end, there can be an analysis of e-Learning cases and scenarios in which these properties become relevant requirements. For instance, we defined privacy trustworthiness fields devoted to publishing student information according to the regulations, responsiveness, and the protection of privacy principles established for each educational institution.

Regarding visualization methods in P2P e-Assessment models, it would be interesting to enhance the proposed visualization tools by conducting additional testing activities. The visualization capabilities for the tutors can be completed with additional facilities, especially those capabilities related to coping with anomalous user identification and integrity.

Although we have tackled the problem of predicting trustworthiness with NN approaches, there are other trustworthiness models without NN methods, such as similarity approaches and collaborative filtering [104,105]. Collaborative filtering is a process of finding similar users, computing predicted ratings, and applying the predictions, such as recommendations to the user [205]. Such approaches can be considered in order to predict student trustworthiness. In this case, the item involved in the recommendation system could be the students themselves, in other words, the collaborative filtered system would be formed by students assessing other students. Then, the recommendation target would be the student's trustworthiness level. From this view, when a collaborative filtering system generates predictions for a target user, the system first identifies the other users whose interests correlate to the target user (ie, user's neighbors). For instance, we could consider that if a tutor performs manual assessment, those students who are the tutor's neighbors, would be trustworthy students. These statements have not been applied and validated in the context of trustworthiness prediction in e-Assessment, thus we propose to tackle the problem of predicting trustworthiness with an innovative collaborative filtering approach, which will be validated in our real e-Learning context.

We were able to carry out several experiments by adapting the model to the design cycles proposed in the methodology. However, we have not extended the application of the methodology to larger scales. Therefore it would be interesting to propose a real online e-Assessment model in a massive learning activity, such as in the contexts of MOOCs.

Regarding the student profile, extending the evaluation and testing to our student profile model in various real online courses all together would give further insights. Since these deployments will require large amount of data analysis, analyzing, and monitoring, the critical mass related to the students community in a sustainable fashion are really challenging issues.

The analysis and the application of a trustworthiness methodology are topics that extend the scope of e-Assessment and CSCL. In this context, there is room for new applications where trustworthiness evaluation and prediction are suitable methods involved in security processes. In particular, future research work should extend to social networks and how to enhance security requirements in this context based on trustworthiness solutions.

Moreover, we are aware of the special relevance that technological security solutions, such as PKI or biometry, had represented in many IT systems. Therefore we also plan to investigate hybrid models based on technological and functional approaches. We believe that trustworthiness and PKI-based approaches potentially form a comprehensive and solid security solution. In this sense, we also plan to consider the relationships between both approaches, that is, how trustworthiness affects PKI and how PKI involves trustworthiness.

Finally, regarding the Hadoop implementation, more advanced components in our framework can be implemented and analyzed to make the implementation more adaptive to heterogeneous clusters. The Apache Hadoop project has recently evolved into a wide variety of specialized and advanced modules, services, and components. Namely, it would be interesting to consider Hive as an abstraction layer language for analyzing data in Hadoop, Pig for scripting instead of Java programming, and Spark as the successor to MapReduce in Hadoop.

Glossary

Anomalous user assessment is an assessment result that is not conclusive and requires further investigation in order to prevent authenticity flaws in the student assessment results

Apache Hadoop software library is a framework devoted to processing of large data sets across distributed clusters of computers using simple programming models

API Application program interface

BSCW Basic support for cooperative work

CA Continuous assessment

CIA Collective intelligence application

CMS Content management system

Collective intelligence is a group or shared intelligence that emerges from the collaboration and or competition of many entities, either human or digital

CSCL Computer-supported collaborative learning

CSV Comma separated values

DBLP Digital Bibliography and Library Project

DNS Domain name system

EDM Educational data mining

EML Educational modeling languages

FMTD Filler mean target difference

HDFS Hadoop distributed file system

HPC High-performance computing

HTTP Hypertext transfer protocol

ICE Information and communication technologies

IDE Integrated development environment

IMS Instructional management system

Information security is the condition of a system that results from the establishment and maintenance of the following properties: availability, integrity, confidentiality, access control, identity, authentication, time stamping, nonrepudiation, audit, and failure control

IP Internet protocol

IS Information security

ISMS Information security management system

IT Information technology

JAR Java archive

KM Knowledge management

LA Learning analytics

LAK Learning analytics and knowledge

Learning management system is a broad term that is used for a wide range of systems that organize and provide access to online learning services to students, teachers, and administrators

153

LMS Learning management system

MapReduce is a programming model and an associated implementation for processing and generating large data sets

MCSCL Mobile computer-supported collaborative learning

ML Mobile learning

MOOC Massive open online course

MOOC-SIA MOOC smart identity agent

MPI Message passing interface

MRv2 MapReduce 2.0

NN Neural network

OpenMP API OpenMP application program interface

P2P Peer-to-peer

PBL Project-based learning

Peer-to-peer e-Assessment is an assessment model where students mutually evaluate peer's activities and contribution during the learning process

PgUp Pretty good privacy

PKI Public key infrastructure

PKIX Internet X.509 public key infrastructure

Public key infrastructure is an infrastructure that allows for the creation of a trusted method for providing privacy, authentication, integrity, and nonrepudiation in communications between two parties

RDF Resource description framework

RFC Request for comments

SCLMS Secure collaborative learning management systems

Security attack is an intentional act by which an entity attempts to evade security services and violate the security policy of a system

Security evidence is information generated by the security system in a reliable way that allows for stating a certain security property has been violated

SNA Social network analysis

SQL Structured query language

STP Student trustworthiness profile

TBF Trustworthiness building factor

TDS Trustworthiness data sources

TMM Trustworthiness measurement methodology

TRF Trustworthiness reducing factor

Trustworthiness is a particular level of the subjective probability with which an agent evaluates how another agent (or group of agents) will perform a particular action, before the agent can monitor such action (or independently of agent's capacity ever to be able to monitor it) and in a context in which it affects the agent's own action

Trustworthiness and security methodology is a theoretical approach devoted to offering a guideline for designing and managing security in collaborative online learning activities through trustworthiness evaluation and prediction.

Trustworthiness factors are those behaviors that reduce or build trustworthiness in a collaborative group

Trustworthiness history sequence is a historical record of trustworthiness of grid services with which the requester has traded. It can be denoted with an ordered tuple where each component is the trustworthiness score of the transaction between a requester and a service

Trustworthy LMS is an online learning system that contains reliable peer services and useful learning resources

TSM Trustworthiness and security methodology

UML Unified modeling language

UOC Universitat Oberta de Catalunya

WOWA Weighted ordered weighted averaging

XML Extensible markup language

YARN Yet another resource negotiator

Bibliography

[1] T. Koschmann, Paradigm shifts and instructional technology, in: T. Koschmann (Ed.), CSCL: Theory and Practice of an Emerging Paradigm, Lawrence Erlbaum Associates, Mahwah, NJ, 1996, pp. 1–23.

[2] E.R. Weippl, Security in e-Learning, in: H. Bidgoli (Ed.), Handbook of Information Security, Key Concepts, Infrastructure, Standards and Protocols, vol. 1, Wiley, Hoboken, NJ, 2006, pp. 279–293.

[3] C.J. Eibl, Discussion of Information Security in E-Learning, Ph.D. thesis, Universität Siegen, Siegen, Germany, 2010, http://dokumentix.ub.uni-siegen.de/opus/volltexte/2010/444/pdf/eibl.pdf.

[4] CSO Magazine, US Secret Service, 2011 Cybersecurity Watch Survey, Software Engineering Institute CERT Program at Carnegie Mellon University, tech. rep., CSO Magazine, Deloitte, 2011.

[5] Trustwave, 2014 Trustwave Global Security Report, tech. rep., Trustwave, 2014, https://www.trustwave.com/Resources/Library/Documents/2014-Trustwave-Global-Security-Report/.

[6] Moodle, Moodle Security Announcements, 2012, https://moodle.org/mod/forum/view.php?id=7128.

[7] Equipo de Serguridad de RedIRIS, Informe de incidentes de seguridad a no 2012, tech. rep., Red Académica y de Investigación Espa nola (RedIRIS), 2013.

[8] S. Píriz, J.P. Gumbau, T. Jiménez, Universitic 2013: situación actual de las TIC en el sistema universitario espa nol, in: Proceedings of Conferencia de Rectores de las Universidades Espa nolas (CRUE), 2013, pp. 1–119.

[9] M.J. Dark, Information Assurance and Security Ethics in Complex Systems: Interdisciplinary Perspectives, Information Science Reference, Hershey, PA, 2011.

[10] S.P. Marsh, Formalising Trust as a Computational Concept, Ph.D. thesis, University of Stirling, 1994.

[11] P. Bernthal, A survey of trust in the workplace, Executive Summary, HR Benchmark Group, Pittsburgh, PA, 1997.

[12] O. Hussain, E. Chang, F. Hussain, T. Dillon, Determining the failure level for risk analysis in an e-commerce interaction, in: T. Dillon, E. Chang, R. Meersman, K. Sycara (Eds.), Advances in Web Semantics I, Lecture Notes in Computer Science, vol. 4891, Springer, Berlin, Heidelberg, 2009, pp. 290–323.

[13] G. Carullo, A. Castiglione, G. Cattaneo, A.D. Santis, U. Fiore, F. Palmieri, Feel-Trust: providing trustworthy communications in ubiquitous mobile environment, in: Proceedings of 2013 IEEE 27th International Conference on Advanced Information Networking and Applications (AINA), Barcelona, Spain, 2013, pp. 1113–1120, http://dx.doi.org/10.1109/AINA.2013.100.

[14] P. Dillenbourg, What do you mean by collaborative learning?, in: P. Dillenbourg (Ed.), Collaborative-Learning: Cognitive and Computational Approaches, Elsevier Science, Oxford, UK, 1999, pp. 1–19.

[15] K.M. Apampa, G. Wills, D. Argles, An approach to presence verification in summative e-Assessment security, in: Proceedings of 2010 International Conference on Information Society (i-Society 2010), IEEE Computer Society, London, UK, 2010, pp. 449–454.

[16] Y. Levy, M. Ramim, A theoretical approach for biometrics authentication of e-Exams, in: Proceedings of Chais Conference on Instructional Technologies Research, The Open University of Israel, Raanana, Israel, 2006, pp. 93–101.

[17] S.K. Ferencz, C.W. Goldsmith, Privacy issues in a virtual learning environment, in: Cause/Effect, A Practitioner's Journal About Managing and Using Information Resources on College and University Campuses, vol. 21, CAUSE, 1998, pp. 5–11, http://net.educause.edu/ir/library/html/cem/cem98/cem9812.html.

[18] C. Yang, F.O. Lin, H. Lin, Policy-based privacy and security management for collaborative e-Education systems, in: Proceedings of 5th IASTED International Multi-Conference Computers and Advanced Technology in Education (CATE 2002), ACTA Press, Cancun, Mexico, 2002, pp. 501–505.

[19] K. El-Khatib, L. Korba, Y. Xu, G. Yee, Privacy and security in e-Learning, Int. J. Dist. Educ. 1 (4) (2003) 174–190.

[20] T. Klobučar, M. Jenabi, A. Kaibel, A. Karapidis, Security and privacy issues in technology—enhanced learning, Knowl. Creat. Diffus. Utili. (2007) 1233–1240, http://www.e5.ijs.si/images/papers/survey_results.pdf.

[21] M. Anwar, J. Greer, Reputation management in privacy—enhanced e-Learning, in: Proceedings of 3rd Annual Scientific Conference of the LORNET Research Network (I2LOR06), ARIES Publications, Montreal, Canada, 2006, pp. 681–683.

[22] W. Hommel, Security and privacy management for learning management systems, in: Learning Management System Technologies and Software Solutions for Online Teaching: Tools and Applications, Information Science Reference, Hershey, PA, 2010, pp. 37–57.

[23] M. Madeth, G. Sébastien, Privacy concerns in e-Learning: is using tracking system a threat?, Int. J. Inform. Educ. Tech. 1 (1) (2011) 1–8.

[24] J. Pei, How to solve the security and privacy problems within e-Learning, in: ITME 2011 Third International Symposium on IT in Medicine and Education, IEEE Computer Society, Guangzhou, China, 2011, pp. 66–69.

[25] J. Yong, Digital identity design and privacy preservation for e-learning, in: Proceedings of 2007 11th International Conference on Computer Supported Cooperative Work in Design, IEEE Computer Society, Melbourne, Australia, 2007, pp. 858–863.

[26] B. Gelbord, On the use of PKI technologies for secure and private e-Learning environments, in: Proceedings of 4th International Conference on Computer Systems and Technologies: e-Learning (CompSysTech), Association for Computing Machinery, Sofia, Bulgaria, 2003, pp. 568–572.

[27] G. Kambourakis, D.P.N. Kontoni, I. Sapounas, Introducing attribute certificates to secure distributed e-Learning or m-learning services, in: V. Uskov (Ed.), Proceedings of IASTED International Conference on Web-based Education—WBE 2004, IASTED, Innsbruck, Australia, 2004, pp. 436–440.

[28] G. Kambourakis, D.-P.N. Kontoni, A. Rouskas, S. Gritzalis, A PKI approach for deploying modern secure distributed e-Learning and m-learning environments, Comput. Educ. 48 (1) (2007) 1–16.

[29] K.M. Apampa, Presence Verification for Summative e-Assessments, Ph.D. thesis, University of Southampton, Southampton, England, 2010.

[30] J. Castella-Roca, J. Herrera-Joancomarti, A. Dorca-Josa, A secure e-Exam management system, in: Proceedings of First International Conference on Availability, Reliability and Security, ARES '06, IEEE Computer Society, Washington, DC, 2006, pp. 864–871, http://dx.doi.org/10.1109/ARES.2006.14.

[31] A. Sabic, J. Azemovic, Model of efficient assessment system with accent on privacy, security and integration with e-University components, in: Proceedings of 2nd International Conference on Education Technology and Computer (ICETC), vol. 3, IEEE Computer Society, Shanghai, China. 2010, pp. 128–131.

[32] A. Bryden, Open and global standards for achieving an inclusive information society, in: Proceedings of 2013 Slovenian Institute for Standardization SIST Conference, Ljubljana, Slovenia, 2003, pp. 1–11, http://www.iso.org/iso/livelinkgetfile?llNodeId=21921&llVolId=-2000.

[33] IMS, IMS Global Learning Consortium, 2015, https://www.imsglobal.org/.

[34] IMS, Final Specification of IMS Learner Information Package Information Model, 2001, http://www.imsglobal.org/profiles/lipinfo01.html.

[35] ISO/IEC, ISO/IEC 17799:2005 (E): Information Technology-Security Techniques-Code of Practice for Information Security Management, 2005.

[36] L. McLaughlin, Interview: Holistic Security, IEEE Security Privacy 3 (3) (2005) 6–8.

[37] ISO/IEC, ISO/IEC 27001:2005(E): Information Technology-Security Techniques-Information Security Management Systems-Requirements, 2005.

[38] J.D. Demott, A. Sotirov, J. Long, Gray Hat Hacking, Third Edition Reviews, third ed., McGraw-Hill Companies, New York, 2011.

[39] Z. Wu, Y. Ou, Y. Liu, A taxonomy of network and computer attacks based on responses, in: Proceedings of 2011 International Conference on Information Technology, Computer Engineering and Management Sciences (ICM), vol. 1, 2011, pp. 26–29.

[40] R. Shirey, RFC 4949: Internet Security Glossary, Version 2, tech. rep., The Internet Engineering Task Force, 2007, http://tools.ietf.org/html/rfc4949.

[41] World Economic Forum, Global Risks 2014, ninth ed., WEF, Geneva, 2014.

[42] S. Harris, All-In-One CISSP Certification Exam Guide, McGraw-Hill Osborne Media, New York, 2002.

[43] D. Parker, Toward a new framework for information security, in: The Computer Security Handbook, fourth ed., Wiley, New York, 2002, pp. 118–137.

[44] W.R. Cheswick, S.M. Bellovin, A.D. Rubin, Firewalls and Internet Security: Repelling the Wily Hacker, Addison-Wesley, Boston, MA, 2003.

[45] K. Raina, PKI Security Solutions for the Enterprise: Solving HIPAA, e-Paper Act, and Other Compliance Issues, Wiley, Indianapolis, IN, 2003.

[46] IETF, Internet Engineering Task Force, 2011, http://www.ietf.org/.

[47] J. Mwakalinga, S. Kowalski, L. Yngstrom, Secure e-Learning using a holistic and immune security framework, in: Proceedings of International Conference for Internet Technology and Secured Transactions, ICITST-2009, 2009, pp. 1–6.

[48] P. Laforcade, Towards a UML-based educational modeling language, in: Proceedings of Fifth IEEE International Conference on Advanced Learning Technologies (ICALT-2005), 2005, pp. 855–859, http://dx.doi.org/10.1109/ICALT.2005.288.

[49] S. Lincke, T. Knautz, M. Lowery, Designing system security with UML misuse deployment diagrams, in: 2012 IEEE Sixth International Conference on Software Security and Reliability Companion (SERE-C), 2012, pp. 57–61, http://dx.doi.org/10.1109/SERE-C.2012.12.

[50] M. Flate, Online education systems: discussion and definition of terms, NKI Dist. Educ., 2002, http://www.porto.ucp.pt/open/curso/modulos/doc/Definition%20of%20Terms.pdf.

[51] S. Caballé, J. Feldman, CoLPE: communities of learning practice environment, in: D. Foster, D. Schuler (Eds.), Proceedings of the Directions and Implications of Advanced Computing, Berkeley, CA, 2008, pp. 35–46.

[52] Moodle, The Moodle Project, 2015, https://moodle.org/.

[53] B. Davis, C. Carmean, E. Wagner, The Evolution of the LMS: From Management to Learning-Deep Analysis of Trends Shaping the Future of eLearning, eLearningGuild Research, Santa Rosa, CA, 2009.

[54] J.C.G. Hernández, M.A.L. Chávez, Moodle security vulnerabilities, in: Proceedings of 5th International Conference on Electrical Engineering, Computing Science and Automatic Control (CCE 2008), IEEE Computer Society, Mexico City, Mexico, 2008, pp. 352–357.

[55] J. Diaz, D. Arroyo, F.B. Rodriguez, An approach for adapting Moodle into a secure infrastructure, in: Proceedings of 4th International Conference on Computational Intelligence in Security for Information Systems CISIS 2011, Springer, Torremolinos, Málaga, Spain, 2011, pp. 214–221.

[56] S. Kumar, K. Dutta, Investigation on security in LMS Moodle, Int. J. Informat. Tech. Knowl. Manag. 4 (1) (2011) 233–238.

[57] G. Stahl, Contributions to a theoretical framework for CSCL, in: Proceedings of the Conference on Computer Support for Collaborative Learning: Foundations for a CSCL Community, CSCL '02, International Society of the Learning Sciences, Boulder, CO, 2002, pp. 62–71, http://0-dl.acm.org.cataleg.uoc.edu/citation.cfm?id=1658616. 1658626.

[58] J. Zumbach, A. Hillers, P. Reimann, Supporting distributed problem-based learning: the use of feedback mechanisms in outline learning, in: T.S. Roberts (Ed.), Online Collaborative Learning: Theory and Practice, Information Science, Hershey, PA, 2004, pp. 86–102.

[59] C.J. Eibl, S. Schubert, Development of e-Learning design criteria with secure realization concepts, in: Proceedings of 3rd International Conference ISSEP—Informatics in Secondary Schools—Evaluation and Perspectives, Springer, Toruń, Poland, 2008, pp. 327–336.

[60] Z. Luo, T. Zhang, A mobile service platform for trustworthy e-Learning service provisioning, in: S. Caballé, F. Xhafa, T. Daradoumis, A.A. Juan, Z. Luo, T. Zhang (Eds.), Architectures for Distributed and Complex M-Learning Systems, IGI Global, 2009, pp. 108–122, http://services.igi-global.com/resolvedoi/resolve.aspx?doi=10.4018/978-1-60566-882-6.

[61] S. Caballé, F. Xhafa, L. Barolli, Using mobile devices to support online collaborative learning, Mob. Inf. Syst. 6 (1) (2010) 27–47, http://dl.acm.org/citation.cfm?id=1804707.1804710.

[62] M. Sharples, J. Taylor, G. Vavoula, Towards a theory of mobile learning, Proc. mLearn 1 (1) (2005) 1–9.

[63] Y. Laouris, N. Eteokleous, We need an educationally relevant definition of mobile learning, in: Proc. mLearn, Cape Town, 2005, pp. 1–13.

[64] J. Sathyan, M. Sadasivan, Multi-layered collaborative approach to address enterprise mobile security challenges, in: Proceedings of IEEE 2nd Workshop on Collaborative Security Technologies (CoSec 2010), 2010, pp. 1–6, http://dx.doi.org/10.1109/COSEC. 2010.5730691.

[65] L. Pappano, The Year of the MOOC, 2012, http://nyti.ms/18ndoGr.

[66] C. Stewart, J. Da Ros, MOOC (Massive Open Online Course), 2013, http://etec.ctlt. ubc.ca/510wiki/MOOC_%28Massive_Open_Online_Course%29.

[67] MIT, MIT OpenCourseWare, 2015, http://ocw.mit.edu/index.htm.

[68] A. McAuley, B. Stewart, G. Siemens, D. Cormier, The MOOC model for digital practice, elearnspace (2010) 1–64, http://www.elearnspace.org/Articles/MOOC_Final.pdf.

[69] K. Pisutova, Open education, in: Proceedings of 2012 IEEE 10th International Conference on Emerging eLearning Technologies Applications (ICETA), 2012, pp. 297–300, http://dx.doi.org/10.1109/ICETA.2012.6418317.

[70] P. Hill, Four Barriers That MOOCs Must Overcome To Build a Sustainable Model, 2012, http://mfeldstein.com/four-barriers-that-moocs-must%0020-overcome-to-become-sustainable-model/.

[71] Coursera Team, Introducing Signature Track, 2015, http://blog.coursera.org/post/40080531667/signaturetrack.

[72] R. Tracey, The future of MOOCs, 2013, http://ryan2point0.wordpress.com/2012/11/26/the-future-of-moocs/.

[73] L. Hardesty, Is MIT giving away the farm?, 2012, http://www.technologyreview.com/article/428698/is-mit-giving-away-the-farm/.

[74] The Princeton EDGE lab, Innovating Education with MOOC/FLIP, 2013, http://scenic.princeton.edu/files/MOOC_FLIP_thoughts.pdf.

[75] M.J. Chapple, N. Chawla, A. Striegel, Authentication anomaly detection: a case study on a virtual private network, in: Proceedings of the Third Annual ACM Workshop on Mining Network Data, MineNet '07, ACM, New York, 2007, pp. 17–22, http://dx.doi.org/10.1145/1269880.1269886.

[76] UOC, University of Catalonia, 2015, http://www.uoc.edu.

[77] A. Sangrà, A new learning model for the information and knowledge society: the case of the Universitat Oberta de Catalunya (UOC), Spain, Int. Rev. Res. Open Distrib. Learn. 2 (2) (2002) 19, http://www.irrodl.org/index.php/irrodl/article/viewArticle/55.

[78] M. Mazzara, L. Biselli, P.P. Greco, N. Dragoni, A. Marraffa, N. Qamar, S. de Nicola, Social networks and collective intelligence: a return to the Agora, in: Social Network Engineering for Secure Web Data and Services, IGI Global, Hershey, PA, 2013, pp. 88–113, http://dx.doi.org/10.4018/978-1-4666-3926-3.ch005.

[79] L. Longo, P. Dondio, S. Barrett, Enhancing social search: a computational collective intelligence model of behavioural traits, trust and time, in: N. Nguyen, R. Kowalczyk (Eds.), Transactions on Computational Collective Intelligence II, Lecture Notes in Computer Science, vol. 6450, Springer, Berlin, Heidelberg, 2010, pp. 46–69.

[80] V. Robu, H. Halpin, H. Shepherd, Emergence of consensus and shared vocabularies in collaborative tagging systems, ACM Trans. Web 3 (4) (2009) 14:1–14:34, http://dx.doi.org/10.1145/1594173.1594176.

[81] D. Gambetta, Can we trust trust?, in: Trust: Making and Breaking Cooperative Relations, Blackwell, Oxford, 1988, pp. 213–237.

[82] M. Raza, F.K. Hussain, O.K. Hussain, Neural network-based approach for predicting trust values based on non-uniform input in mobile applications, Comput. J. 55 (3) (2012) 347–378, http://dx.doi.org/10.1093/comjnl/bxr104.

[83] RDF Working Group, Resource Description Framework (RDF), 2014, http://www.w3.org/RDF/.

[84] O. Hartig, Trustworthiness of data on the web, in: STI Berlin CSW PhD Workshop, Humboldt-Universität zu Berlin, German, 2008, pp. 1–5.

[85] C. Dai, D. Lin, E. Bertino, M. Kantarcioglu, An approach to evaluate data trustworthiness based on data provenance, in: W. Jonker, M. Petković (Eds.), Secure Data Management, vol. 5159, Springer, Berlin, Heidelberg, 2008, pp. 82–98.

[86] Y. Liu, Y. Wu, A survey on trust and trustworthy e-Learning system, in: Proceedings of 2010 International Conference on Web Information Systems and Mining, IEEE, 2010, pp. 118–122, http://dx.doi.org/10.1109/WISM.2010.62.

[87] J. Miguel, S. Caballé, F. Xhafa, J. Prieto, L. Barolli, A methodological approach to modelling trustworthiness in online collaborative learning, in: Proceedings of Fourth International Workshop on Adaptive Learning via Interactive, Collaborative and Emotional Approaches (ALICE 2014), IEEE Computer Society, Salerno, Italy, 2014, pp. 451–456, http://dx.doi.org/10.1109/INCoS.2014.18.

[88] J. Miguel, S. Caballé, F. Xhafa, J. Prieto, Security in online assessments: towards an effective trustworthiness approach to support e-learning teams, in: Proceedings of 28th International Conference on Advanced Information Networking and Applications (AINA 2014), IEEE Computer Society, Victoria, Canada, 2014, pp. 123–130, http://dx.doi.org/10.1109/AINA.2014.106.

[89] J. Miguel, S. Caballé, F. Xhafa, J. Prieto, L. Barolli, A methodological approach for trustworthiness assessment and prediction in mobile online collaborative learning, Comput. Stand. Interfaces 44 (2015) 122–136, http://dx.doi.org/10.1016/j.csi.2015.04.008.

[90] J. Miguel, S. Caballé, F. Xhafa, J. Prieto, L. Barolli, Predicting trustworthiness behavior to enhance security in on-line assessment, in: Proceedings of 6th International Conference on Intelligent Networking and Collaborative Systems (INCoS 2014), IEEE Computer Society, Salerno, Italy, 2014, pp. 342–349, http://dx.doi.org/10.1109/INCoS.2014.19.

[91] Y. Liu, D. Chen, J. Sun, A trustworthy e-Learning based on trust and quality evaluation, in: Proceedings of 2011 International Conference on E-Business and E-Government (ICEE), 2011, pp. 1–4, http://dx.doi.org/10.1109/ICEBEG.2011.5881690.

[92] J. Champaign, R. Cohen, Modeling trustworthiness of peer advice in a framework for presenting web objects that supports peer commentary, in: Proceedings of 20th Conference on User Modeling, Adaptation, and Personalization, Montreal, Canada, 2012, pp. 1–12.

[93] S.J.H. Yang, I.Y.L. Chen, Kinshuk, N.-S. Chen, Enhancing the quality of e-Learning in virtual learning communities by finding quality learning content and trustworthy collaborators, Educ. Tech. Soc. 10 (2) (2007) 84–95, http://www.editlib.org/p/75303.

[94] I. Ray, S. Chakraborty, A vector model of trust for developing trustworthy systems, in: D. Hutchison, T. Kanade, J. Kittler, J.M. Kleinberg, F. Mattern, J.C. Mitchell, M. Naor, O. Nierstrasz, C. Pandu Rangan, B. Steffen, M. Sudan, D. Terzopoulos, D. Tygar, M.Y. Vardi, G. Weikum, P. Samarati, P. Ryan, D. Gollmann, R. Molva (Eds.), Computer Security—ESORICS 2004, vol. 3193, Springer, Berlin, Heidelberg, 2004, pp. 260–275.

[95] E. Damiani, S. De Capitani di Vimercati, P. Samarati, M. Viviani, A WOWA-based aggregation technique on trust values connected to metadata, Electron. Notes Theor. Comput. Sci. 157 (3) (2006) 131–142, http://dx.doi.org/10.1016/j.entcs.2005.09.036.

[96] A. Rajaraman, J.D. Ullman, Recommendation systems, in: Mining of Massive Datasets, Cambridge University Press, Cambridge, 2011, pp. 305–339, http://ebooks.cambridge.org/ref/id/CBO9781139058452.

[97] M. Li, Z. Hua, J. Zhao, Y. Zou, B. Xie, ARIMA model-based web services trustworthiness evaluation and prediction, in: C. Liu, H. Ludwig, F. Toumani, Q. Yu (Eds.), Service-Oriented Computing, Lecture Notes in Computer Science, vol. 7636, Springer, Berlin, Heidelberg, 2012, pp. 648–655.

[98] B. Mobasher, R. Burke, R. Bhaumik, C. Williams, Toward trustworthy recommender systems: an analysis of attack models and algorithm robustness, ACM Trans. Internet Technol. (2007) http://dx.doi.org/10.1145/1278366.1278372.

[99] L. Ge, J. Gao, X. Yu, W. Fan, A. Zhang, Estimating local information trustworthiness via multi-source joint matrix factorization, in: Proceedings of 2012 IEEE 12th International Conference on Data Mining (ICDM), Brussels, Belgium, 2012, pp. 876–881, http://dx.doi.org/10.1109/ICDM.2012.151.

[100] S. Msanjila, H. Afsarmanesh, Automating trust assessment for configuration of temporary partnerships, in: A. Azevedo (Ed.), Innovation in Manufacturing Networks, IFIP—The International Federation for Information Processing, vol. 266, Springer, New York, 2008, pp. 95–104.

[101] Z. Zhai, W. Zhang, The estimation of trustworthy of grid services based on neural network, J. Netw. 5 (10) (2010) 1135–1142, http://dblp.uni-trier.de/db/journals/jnw/jnw5.html#ZhaiZ10.

[102] K. Konrad, G. Fuchs, J. Barthel, Trust and electronic commerce-more than a technical problem, in: Proceedings of the 18th IEEE Symposium on Reliable Distributed Systems, 1999, pp. 360–365, http://dx.doi.org/10.1109/RELDIS.1999.805124.

[103] W. Song, V. Phoha, X. Xu, An adaptive recommendation trust model in multiagent system, in: Proceedings of IEEE/WIC/ACM International Conference on Intelligent Agent Technology (IAT 2004), Beijing, China, 2004, pp. 462–465, http://dx.doi.org/10.1109/IAT.2004.1342996.

[104] A.J. Flanagin, M.J. Metzger, Trusting expert- versus user-generated ratings online: the role of information volume, valence, and consumer characteristics, Comput. Human Behav. 29 (4) (2013) 1626–1634, http://dx.doi.org/10.1016/j.chb.2013.02.001.

[105] X. Liu, A. Datta, A trust prediction approach capturing agents' dynamic behavior, in: Proceedings of Twenty-Second International Joint Conference on Artificial Intelligence, IJCAI'11, AAAI Press, Barcelona, Catalonia, Spain, 2011, pp. 2147–2152, http://dx.doi.org/10.5591/978-1-57735-516-8/IJCAI11-358.

[106] F. Hussain, O. Hussain, E. Chang, Trustworthiness measurement methodology (tmm) for assessment purposes, in: Proceedings of IEEE International Conference on Computational Cybernetics ICCC-2007, Gammarth, Tunisia, 2007, pp. 107–112, http://dx.doi.org/10.1109/ICCCYB.2007.4402024.

[107] M. Carbone, M. Nielsen, V. Sassone, A formal model for trust in dynamic networks, in: Proceedings of Third IEEE International Conference on Software Engineering and Formal Methods, Society Press, Los Alamitos, CA, 2003, pp. 54–63, http://dx.doi.org/10.1109/SEFM.2003.1236207.

[108] M. Wojcik, J. Eloff, H. Venter, Trust model architecture: defining prejudice by learning, in: S. Fischer-Hübner, S. Furnell, C. Lambrinoudakis (Eds.), Trust and Privacy in Digital Business, Lecture Notes in Computer Science, vol. 4083, Springer, Berlin, Heidelberg, 2006, pp. 182–191.

[109] S. Caballé, T. Daradoumis, F. Xhafa, J. Conesa, Enhancing knowledge management in online collaborative learning, Int. J. Softw. Eng. Knowl. Eng. 20 (4) (2010) 485–497, http://dx.doi.org/10.1142/S0218194010004839.

[110] E. Sallis, G. Jones, Knowledge Management in Education: Enhancing Learning & Education, Kogan Page, London, Sterling, VA, 2002.

[111] W. Omona, T. van der Weide, J.T. Lubega, Using ICT to enhance knowledge management in higher education: a conceptual framework and research agenda, Int. J. Educ. Dev. Using ICT 6 (4) (2010) 83–101.

[112] S. Caballé, T. Daradoumis, F. Xhafa, Efficient embedding of information and knowledge into CSCL applications, in: K.-C. Hui, Z. Pan, R.-K. Chung, C. Wang, X. Jin, S. Göbel, E.-L. Li (Eds.), Technologies for E-Learning and Digital Entertainment, Lecture Notes in Computer Science, vol. 4469, Springer, Berlin, Heidelberg, 2007, pp. 548–559.

[113] S. Narkhede, T. Baraskar, HMR log analyzer: analyze web application logs over Hadoop MapReduce, Int. J. UbiComp 4 (3) (2013) 41–51, http://dx.doi.org/10.5121/iju.2013.4304.

[114] S. Caballé, C. Paniagua, F. Xhafa, T. Daradoumis, A grid-aware implementation for providing effective feedback to on-line learning groups, in: R. Meersman, Z. Tari, P. Herrero (Eds.), On the Move to Meaningful Internet Systems 2005: OTM 2005 Workshops, Lecture Notes in Computer Science, vol. 3762, Springer, Berlin, Heidelberg, Agia Napa, Cyprus, 2005, pp. 274–283.

[115] S. Caballe, F. Xhafa, T. Daradoumis, A grid approach to efficiently embed information and knowledge about group activity into collaborative learning applications, in: The Learning Grid Handbook, vol. 2, IOS Press, Amsterdam, The Netherlands, 2008, pp. 173–197.

[116] F. Xhafa, C. Paniagua, L. Barolli, S. Caballe, A parallel grid-based implementation for real-time processing of event log data of collaborative applications, Int. J. Web Grid Serv. 6 (2) (2010) 124–140, http://dx.doi.org/10.1504/IJWGS.2010.033788.

[117] The Apache Software Foundation, The Apache Hadoop project, 2015, https://hadoop.apache.org/.

[118] J. Dean, S. Ghemawat, MapReduce: simplified data processing on large clusters, in: Proceedings of Sixth Symposium on Operating System Design and Implementation (OSDI 2004), San Francisco, CA, 2004, pp. 1–13.

[119] T. White, Hadoop: The Definitive Guide, third ed., O'Reilly, Beijing, 2012.

[120] G. Siemens, R.S.J.D. Baker, Learning analytics and educational data mining: towards communication and collaboration, in: Proceedings of 2nd International Conference on Learning Analytics and Knowledge, LAK '12, ACM, New York, 2012, pp. 252–254, http://dx.doi.org/10.1145/2330601.2330661.

[121] C. Romero, S. Ventura, Data mining in education, Wiley Interdiscipl. Rev.: Data Mining Knowl. Discov. 3 (1) (2013) 12–27, http://dx.doi.org/10.1002/widm.1075.

[122] C. Romero (Ed.), Handbook of Educational Data Mining, Chapman & Hall/CRC Data Mining and Knowledge Discovery Series, CRC Press, Boca Raton, FL, 2011.

[123] C. Romero, S. Ventura, E. Garcia, C. de Castro, M. Gea, Collaborative data mining tool for education, in: Proceedings of 2nd International Conference on Educational Data Mining Educational Data Mining (EDM 2009), Cordoba, Spain, 2009, pp. 299–308.

[124] J. Han, Y. Sun, X. Yan, P. Yu, Mining knowledge from data: an information network analysis approach, in: Proceedings of 2012 IEEE 28th International Conference on Data Engineering (ICDE), Washington, DC, 2012, pp. 1214–1217, http://dx.doi.org/10.1109/ICDE.2012.145.

[125] University of Lugano, The GISMO project, 2015, http://gismo.sourceforge.net/.

[126] LOCO-Analyst, The LOCO-Analyst tool, 2015, http://jelenajovanovic.net/LOCO-Analyst.

[127] Pittsburgh Science of Learning Center, The PSLC DataShop services, 2012, http://pslcdatashop.web.cmu.edu/.

[128] Alberta Innovates Centre for Machine Learning, The Meerkat-ED tool, 2015, http://webdocs.cs.ualberta.ca/rabbanyk/MeerkatED/.

[129] Cytoscape Consortium, The Cytoscape Platform, 2015, http://www.cytoscape.org.

[130] Association Gephi, The Open Graph Viz Platform, 2015, https://gephi.github.io/.

[131] S. Boccaletti, V. Latora, Y. Moreno, M. Chavez, D.-U. Hwang, Complex networks: structure and dynamics, Phys. Rep. 424 (4–5) (2006) 175–308, http://dx.doi.org/10.1016/j.physrep.2005.10.009.

[132] R. Ackland, D.L. Hansen, B. Shneiderman, M.A. Smith, Analyzing Social Media Networks With NodeXL: Insights From a Connected World, Elsevier, Morgan Kaufmann, Burlington, 2011, http://site.ebrary.com/lib/alltitles/docDetail.action?docID=10408229.

[133] M. Kudelka, Z. Horak, V. Snasel, A. Abraham, Social network reduction based on stability, in: Proceedings of 2010 International Conference on Computational Aspects of Social Networks (CASoN), Taiyuan, China, 2010, pp. 509–514, http://dx.doi.org/10.1109/CASoN.2010.120.

[134] B. Schneier, Beyond Fear: Thinking Sensibly About Security in an Uncertain World, Copernicus Books, New York, 2003.

[135] R. West, The psychology of security, Commun. ACM 51 (4) (2008) 34–40, http://dx.doi.org/10.1145/1330311.1330320.

[136] L. Rasmusson, S. Jansson, Simulated social control for secure Internet commerce, in: Proceedings of the 1996 Workshop on New Security Paradigms, NSPW '96, ACM, New York, 1996, pp. 18–25, http://dx.doi.org/10.1145/304851.304857.

[137] A. Abdul-Rahman, S. Hailes, Using recommendations for managing trust in distributed systems, in: Proceedings of IEEE Intl. Conference on Communication, Malaysia, 1997, pp. 1–7.

[138] UOC, About the UOC—Educational model, 2016, http://www.uoc.edu/portal/en/universitat/model-educatiu/index.html.

[139] J. Miguel, S. Caballé, F. Xhafa, J. Prieto, L. Barolli, A collective intelligence approach for building student's trustworthiness profile in online learning, in: Proceedings of Ninth International Conference on P2P, Parallel, Grid, Cloud and Internet Computing (3PGCIC 2014), IEEE Computer Society, Guangzhou, China, 2014, pp. 46–53, http://dx.doi.org/10.1109/3PGCIC.2014.132.

[140] J. Miguel, S. Caballé, F. Xhafa, J. Prieto, L. Barolli, Towards a normalized trustworthiness approach to enhance security in on-line assessment, in: Proceedings of Eighth International Conference on Complex, Intelligent and Software Intensive Systems (CISIS 2014), IEEE Computer Society, Birmingham, UK, 2014, pp. 147–154, http://dx.doi.org/10.1109/CISIS.2014.22.

[141] T. Jonge, R. Veenhoven, L. Arends, Homogenizing responses to different survey questions on the same topic: proposal of a scale homogenization method using a reference distribution, Soc. Indicat. Res. (2013) http://dx.doi.org/10.1007/s11205-013-0335-6.

[142] American Psychological Association, Publication Manual of the American Psychological Association, sixth ed., American Psychological Association, Washington, DC, 2010.

[143] Social Media Research Foundation, NodeXL, 2015, http://nodexl.codeplex.com/.

[144] M.A. Smith, B. Shneiderman, N. Milic-Frayling, E. Mendes Rodrigues, V. Barash, C. Dunne, T. Capone, A. Perer, E. Gleave, Analyzing (social media) networks with NodeXL, in: Proceedings of Fourth International Conference on Communities and Technologies, C&T '09, ACM, New York, 2009, pp. 255–264, http://dx.doi.org/10.1145/1556460.1556497.

[145] Z. Horak, M. Kudelka, V. Snasel, A. Abraham, H. Rezankova, Forcoa.NET: an interactive tool for exploring the significance of authorship networks in DBLP data, in: Proceedings of 2011 International Conference on Computational Aspects of Social Networks (CASoN), 2011, pp. 261–266, http://dx.doi.org/10.1109/CASON.2011.6085955.

[146] J. Solomon, R. Wash, Critical mass of what? Exploring Community Growth in WikiProjects, in: Proceedings of Eighth International AAAI Conference on Weblogs and Social Media, Ann Arbor, MI, 2014, pp. 292–301, http://www.aaai.org/ocs/index.php/ICWSM/ICWSM14/paper/view/8104.

[147] M. Nguyen, D. Tran, A computational trust model with trustworthiness against liars in multiagent systems, in: N.-T. Nguyen, K. Hoang, P. Jedrzejowicz (Eds.), Computational Collective Intelligence. Technologies and Applications, Lecture Notes in Computer Science, vol. 7653, Springer, Berlin, Heidelberg, 2012, pp. 446–455.

[148] D.G. Gregg, Designing for collective intelligence, Commun. ACM53 (4) (2010) 134–138, http://dx.doi.org/10.1145/1721654.1721691.

[149] T. O'Reilly, What is Web 2.0: Design patterns and business models for the next generation of software, 2005, http://www.oreillynet.com/pub/a/oreilly/tim/news/2005/09/30/what-is-web-20.html.

[150] Moodle Community, Moodle Docs, 2015, https://docs.moodle.org.

[151] D. Pérez Marín, E. Alfonseca, P. Rodríguez, On the dynamic adaptation of computer assisted assessment of free-text answers, in: V. Wade, H. Ashman, B. Smyth (Eds.), Adaptive Hypermedia and Adaptive Web-Based Systems, Lecture Notes in Computer Science, vol. 4018, Springer, Berlin Heidelberg, 2005, pp. 374–377.

[152] V. Bresfelean, M. Bresfelean, N. Ghisoiu, C.-A. Comes, Determining students' academic failure profile founded on data mining methods, in: Proceedings of 30th International Conference on Information Technology Interfaces (ITI 2008), Cavtat/Dubrovnik, Croatia, 2008, pp. 317–322, http://dx.doi.org/10.1109/ITI.2008.4588429.

[153] UOC, UOC OpenCourseWare, 2015, http://ocw.uoc.edu/.

[154] Cuerpo Nacional de Policía, Portal del DNI Electronico, 2015, http://www.dnielectronico.es/PortalDNIe/.

[155] V. Ciesielski, A. Lalani, Data mining of web access logs from an academic web site, in: A. Abraham, M. Köppen, K. Franke (Eds.), Design and Application of Hybrid Intelligent Systems, IOS Press, Amsterdam, The Netherlands, 2003, pp. 1034–1043, http://dl.acm.org/citation.cfm?id=998038.998151.

[156] S. Caballé, F. Xhafa, Distributed-based massive processing of activity logs for efficient user modeling in a Virtual Campus, Cluster Computing 16 (6) (2013) 829–844, http://dx.doi.org/10.1007/s10586-013-0256-9.

[157] D.B. Skillicorn, D. Talia, Models and languages for parallel computation, ACM Comput. Surv. 30 (2) (1998) 123–169, http://dx.doi.org/10.1145/280277.280278.

[158] I. Gorton, P. Greenfield, A. Szalay, R. Williams, Data-intensive computing in the 21st century, Computer 41 (4) (2008) 30–32, http://dx.doi.org/10.1109/MC.2008.122.

[159] B. Furht, A. Escalante (Eds.), Handbook of Cloud Computing, Springer US, Boston, MA, 2010, http://link.springer.com/10.1007/978-1-4419-6524-0.

[160] F. Xhafa, W. Rahayu, M. Takizawa, Frontiers in intelligent cloud services, World Wide Web 18 (6) (2015) 1519–1521, http://dx.doi.org/10.1007/s11280-015-0338-0.

[161] L.M. Vaquero, L. Rodero-Merino, J. Caceres, M. Lindner, A break in the clouds: towards a cloud definition, SIGCOMM Comput. Commun. Rev. 39 (1) (2008) 50–55, http://dx.doi.org/10.1145/1496091.1496100.

[162] C. Dobre, F. Xhafa, Parallel programming paradigms and frameworks in big data era, Int. J. Parall. Program. 42 (5) (2014) 710–738, http://dx.doi.org/10.1007/s10766-013-0272-7.

[163] S.J. Kang, S.Y. Lee, K.M. Lee, Performance comparison of OpenMP, MPI, and MapReduce in practical problems, Adv. Multimedia 2015 (2015) 7, http://dx.doi.org/10.1155/2015/575687.

[164] R. Greenlaw, H.J. Hoover, Parallel computation: models and complexity issues, in: M.J. Atallah, M. Blanton (Eds.), Algorithms and Theory of Computation Handbook, vol. 2, Chapman & Hall/CRC, Boca Raton, FL, 2010, p. 28, http://0-dl.acm.org.cataleg.uoc.edu/citation.cfm?id=1882757.1882785.

[165] K. Asanovic, R. Bodik, B.C. Catanzaro, J.J. Gebis, P. Husbands, K. Keutzer, D.A. Patterson, W.L. Plishker, J. Shalf, S.W. Williams, K.A. Yelick, The landscape of parallel computing research: a view from Berkeley, Tech. Rep. UCB/EECS-2006-183, EECS Department, University of California, Berkeley, CA, 2006, http://www.eecs.berkeley.edu/Pubs/TechRpts/2006/EECS-2006-183.html.

[166] PlanetLab Consortium, The PlanetLab platform, 2015, https://www.planet-lab.org.

[167] J. Dean, S. Ghemawat, MapReduce: simplified data processing on large clusters, Commun. ACM 51 (1) (2008) 107–113, http://dx.doi.org/10.1145/1327452.1327492.

[168] H. Karloff, S. Suri, S. Vassilvitskii, A model of computation for MapReduce, in: Proceedings of the Twenty-First Annual ACM-SIAM Symposium on Discrete Algorithms, SODA '10, Society for Industrial and Applied Mathematics, Philadelphia, PA, 2010, pp. 938–948, http://0-dl.acm.org.cataleg.uoc.edu/citation.cfm?id=1873601.1873677.

[169] Apache Community, The Hadoop Wiki, 2015, http://wiki.apache.org/hadoop/PoweredBy.

[170] The Apache Software Foundation, The Apache Hadoop Project, 2014, https://hadoop.apache.org/.

[171] The Apache Software Foundation, Apache Hadoop NextGen MapReduce (YARN), 2015, http://hadoop.apache.org/docs/current/hadoop-yarn/hadoop-yarn-site/YARN.html.

[172] The Apache Software Foundation, HDFS Users Guide, 2015, http://hadoop.apache.org/docs/current/hadoop-project-dist/hadoop-hdfs/HdfsUserGuide.html.

[173] CBS Interactive, Last.fm, 2015, http://www.last.fm/.

[174] Facebook, The Facebook Page, 2015.

[175] Rackspace US, Rackspace Hosting Web Site, 2015, https://www.rackspace.com/.

[176] The Apache Software Foundation, Hadoop Cluster Setup, 2015, http://hadoop.apache.org/docs/current/hadoop-project-dist/hadoop-common/ClusterSetup.html.

[177] The OpenMP Architecture Review Board, OpenMP Application Program Interface, 2013, http://www.openmp.org/mp-documents/OpenMP4.0.0.pdf.

[178] Linux Programmer's Manual, pthreads—POSIX threads, 2015, http://man7.org/linux/man-pages/man7/pthreads.7.html.

[179] Message Passing Interface Forum, MPI: A Message-Passing Interface Standard Version 3.0, tech. rep., Message Passing Interface Forum, 2012, http://www.mpi-forum.org/docs/mpi-3.0/mpi30-report.pdf.

[180] J. Diaz, C. Muñoz Caro, A. Nino, A survey of parallel programming models and tools in the multi and many-core era, IEEE Trans. Parall. Distrib. Syst. 23 (8) (2012) 1369–1386, http://dx.doi.org/10.1109/TPDS.2011.308.

[181] OrbiTeam, BSCW Groupware for efficient team collaboration and document management, 2015, http://www.bscw.de.

[182] The Apache Software Foundation, The Apache HTTP Server Project, 2015, http://httpd.apache.org/.

[183] The Apache Software Foundation, Apache HTTP Server Version 2.2 Documentation, 2014, http://httpd.apache.org/docs/2.2/.

[184] W. Appelt, What groupware functionality do users really use? Analysis of the usage of the BSCW system, in: Proceedings of Ninth Euromicro Workshop on Parallel and Distributed Processing, IEEE Comput. Soc., Mantova, Italy, 2001, pp. 337–341, http://dx.doi.org/10.1109/EMPDP.2001.905060.

[185] Fraunhofer FIT, OrbiTeam Software GmbH & Co. KG, X-BSCW: An XML-RPC API to BSCW, 2012, http://www.bscw.de/files/Download/BSCW50-API.pdf.

[186] Fraunhofer FIT, OrbiTeam Software GmbH & Co. KG, BSCW 5.0 Manual, 2013, http://www.bscw.de/files/Download/Help/bscw_help_50_en_print.pdf.

[187] G. Combs, Wireshark network protocol analyzer, 2015, https://www.wireshark.org/.

[188] F. Salfner, S. Tschirpke, M. Malek, Comprehensive logfiles for autonomic systems, in: Proceedings of 18th International Parallel and Distributed Processing Symposium, 2004, p. 211, http://dx.doi.org/10.1109/IPDPS.2004.1303243.

[189] Polytechnic University of Catalonia, The RDlab, 2015, http://rdlab.cs.upc.edu/index.php/en/.

[190] Oracle Corporation, MySQL, 2015, http://www.mysql.com/.

[191] R. O'Reilly, Emergent neural network simulator, 2014, https://grey.colorado.edu/emergent/index.php/Main_Page.

[192] B. Aisa, B. Mingus, R. O'Reilly, The Emergent neural modeling system, Neural Networks 21 (8) (2008) 1146–1152, http://dx.doi.org/10.1016/j.neunet.2008.06.016.

[193] Google, Google Forms, 2015, https://www.google.com/forms/about/.

[194] C. Schmitz, LimeSurvey Project, 2015, http://www.limesurvey.org.

[195] Super CSV, Super CSV package for Java, 2015, http://super-csv.github.io/super-csv/index.html.

[196] Free Software Foundation, GNU PSPP, 2015, http://www.gnu.org/software/pspp/.

[197] Cloudera, Cloudera Product Documentation, 2015, http://www.cloudera.com/content/cloudera/en/documentation.html.

[198] Eclipse Foundation, The Eclipse Community, 2015, http://www.eclipse.org/.

[199] Oracle Corporation, The NetBeans IDE Project, 2015, https://netbeans.org/.

[200] UPC, Polytechnic University of Catalonia, 2015, http://www.upc.edu/.

[201] Seagate Technology LLC, The Lustre file system, 2015, http://lustre.org/.

[202] RDlab, Cluster Advanced, 2015, http://rdlab.cs.upc.edu/docu/.

[203] T.M.J. Fruchterman, E.M. Reingold, Graph drawing by force-directed placement, Softw. Pract. Exp. 21 (11) (1991) 1129–1164, http://dx.doi.org/10.1002/spe.4380211102.

[204] M. Ley, DBLP XML Requests, 2015, http://dblp.uni-trier.de/xml/.

[205] I. Soboroff, C. Nicholas, Collaborative filtering and the generalized vector space model (poster session), in: Proceedings of 23rd Annual International ACM SIGIR Conference on Research and Development in Information Retrieval, SIGIR '00 ACM, New York, 2000, pp. 351–353, http://dx.doi.org/10.1145/345508.345646.

Index

Note: Page numbers followed by *f* indicate figures and *t* indicate tables.